EX MEDIO CENTRI

EX MEDIO CENTRI

By

Michael Jerry Mitchell

First Edition

Sowsback Society

Olympia

Preface

      The most common questions I am asked are, "Why are you obsessed with mushrooms?", "Do you ever talk about anything else besides mushrooms?", "Are you on mushrooms?", or "Where did you read that?". No, No, No, and No. Mushrooms to me were just a weed that popped up in my mother's front yard, nothing more. I was raised Catholic, not allowed to eat before I said prayer, prayed before I slept, that sort of thing. When I was fourteen I found out I was adopted, I realized that the wool can be pulled over anyone's eyes even regarding their most concrete beliefs and so I started studying and this is what I discovered.

Namaste,
Michael Jerry Mitchell

Table of Contents

Preface...v

Contents...vii

Chapter One...4

Chapter Two...27

Chapter Three..40

Chapter Four..58

Chapter Five...89

Chapter Six..99

Chapter Seven...112

Chapter Eight..134

Chapter Nine...160

Epilogue..178

Bibliography..180

Index..181

(NEVER UNDER ANY CIRCUMSTANCES INGEST DRUGS OF ANY SORT, ANY DRUGS OR PLANTS IN THIS BOOK AND THE MENTIONED USE OF, IS STRICTLY A HISTORICAL REFERENCE AND MUCH SCIENTIFIC AND MEDICAL RESEARCH IS NECESSARY TO KNOW WHAT THE HARMFUL AND DEVASTATING TOXIC EFFECTS OF THESE CHEMICALS ARE! DEATH CAN BE A RESULT, IT IS HIGHLY PROBABLE. LIVER DAMAGE IS FATAL!)

Chapter One: All Things Hidden

"The Pharisees and the Scribes have taken and hidden the sacred keys to acquaintance of oneself and hidden them. They have neither entered nor let those who want to enter do so. You all, then, must be as hidden as snakes and as innocent as doves."

- Jesus Christ

There simply is just too large of plethora of information on the hidden use of drugs in the history of the world to organize articulately a comprehensive study that could be condensed into a single readable book today. So with that said I will note that I have tried however to present information that would help fuel the reader's desire to learn more and provide some information to consider while studying further.

While reading Carl Jung's work I realized that the philosophists were encoding real doctrine in their alchemical texts from the quotes I was examining. You can actually figure out what they are saying if you read the manuscripts from the original and oldest alchemist. For instance, Carl Jung mentions in "Alchemical Studies," "In the Arabic 'Book of Ostanes' there is a description of the arcane substance, or the water, in its various forms, first white, then black, then red, and finally a combustible liquid or a fire which is struck from certain stones in Persia." You see, they say "first" to confuse the reader and make the reader think red, white and black are three various forms and not all colors of one form but put simply the description of the arcane substance is white, black and red and then a tincture form as well. Well the Amanita muscaria mushroom is red and white and black on the bottom after you rip it up and you will see these colors come up a lot for instance in "Rhasis Arabs" by Idem Haly it is written "white and Red proceed from the same root without any other kind intervenient. For it dissolves, and conjoins itself, makes itself black and citrine, white and red, espouses itself, conceives, brings forth, and does all to the perfect end."

   To the fact that the word stones is used I say that mushrooms have long been called little stones on the ground. For instance, "these stones will shout", "he used a stone as a pillow", the "swaddled stone" given to Kronos to free his children is known as the sin-bearing child, the "philosopher's stone", and the "sapphire stone". I'd like to note that sapphire is blueish in color as are psilocybin mushrooms when you touch them and cause bruising to occur. Jung continues, "'The prima materia is an oily water and is the philosophic stone, from which branches multiply into infinity,' says Mylius. Here the stone is itself the tree and is understood as the 'fiery substance' or as 'oily water.' As oil and water do not mix indicative of the dual nature of Mercurius. As a rule, the lapis is synthesized from the quaternity of the elements or from the ogdoad of elements plus qualities (cold/warm, moist/dry). Similarly Mercurius, known from ancient times as quadratus, is the arcane substance through whose transformation the lapis, or goal of the opus, is produced... the stone is itself depicted there as the tree of life and the 'fiery substance.'"

"The fruits of the philosophical tree drop off, and the tree itself dies and vanishes in the Earth. Afterwards, in accordance with natural conditions, another new tree is there."
- "De genealogia mineralium," Theatre. Chem., I (1659) p. 574.

"When the body is dissolved, there will sometimes appear two branches, sometimes three, sometimes more..."
- Theatre. Chem., I (1659) p. 147f.

"The salt and the tree can be made in any moist and convenient place."
-Gloria Mundi, Mus. herm., p. 216

In the beginning, it was said, when Zeus had first come into the kingdom of the universe, he had sought to measure the scale of his inheritance by releasing one eagle from the east and one from the west, and watching them fly, to locate the center of the world. The two birds had met at Delphi, and a great egg of rock, the "Navel Stone," or Omphalos, marks the spot. At Delphi, for nine months every year, the Lord Apollo was believed to have his dwelling. Delphi was indeed the most sacred spot in all of Greece; there was no other oracle to compare with it.

Dan Russell in "Shamanism and Drug Propaganda the Patriarchy and the Drug War" chimes in with,"The connection of the lapis with immortality is attested from very early times. Ostanes (possibly 4th cent. B.C.) speaks of 'the Nile stone that has a spirit.' The lapis is the panacea, the universal medicine, the alexipharmic, the tincture... It brings riches, power, and health; it cures melancholy and, as the vivus lapis philosophicus, is a symbol of the saviour, the Anthropos, and immortality."

Haly says, "Our stone is life to him who knows it and how it is made, and he who knows not and has not made it and to whom no assurance is given when it will be born, or who thinks it another stone, has already prepared himself for death." So here we see Haly mentioning what has happened to so many would-be self-initiates, they perish from taking the wrong mushroom. Please remember that the goal of the opus is the lapis. I will tell you now that the lapis or the goal of the opus is realizing that you are one with the universe. Many have spiritual experiences when they experience mushrooms or a good experience turns bad because their bodies cannot handle the amount of adrenaline for the duration of the experience if at all in the beginning.

Wei Po-yang, the oldest Chinese alchemist known to us (2nd century A.D.), gives an instructive account of the dangerous consequences of making mistakes during the opus. Wei Po-yang gives a graphic description of the physiological and psychic consequences of error: "Gases from food consumed will make noises inside the intestines and stomach... Days and nights will be passed without sleep, moon after moon. The body will then be tired out, giving rise to an appearance of insanity. The hundred pulses will stir and boil so violently as to drive away peace of mind and body. Ghostly things will make their appearance, at which he will marvel even in his sleep. He is then led to rejoice, thinking that he is assured of longevity. But all of a sudden he is seized by an untimely death. A slight error has thus led to a grave disaster."

This is obviously a description of a mushroom poisoning. The part where the victim is led to rejoice all the while dying a short time later really tops it off as it takes a little while for you to die from liver failure. There is a 15th century alchemical manuscript and here is what Wikipedia has to say about it, "The 'Aurora consurgens' is an illuminated manuscript of the 15th century in the Zürich Zentralbibliothek. It contains a medieval alchemical treatise, in the past sometimes attributed to Thomas Aquinas, now to a writer called the 'Pseudo-Aquinas.' Unusually for a work of this type, the manuscript contains thirty-eight fine miniatures in watercolour. The illustrations are allegorical representations of alchemical elements depicted in human or animal form. For example, mercury is depicted as a serpent; gold as the Sun and silver as the Moon."

Quoting from the "Aurora consurgens I", in regard to the dangers which threaten the artifex: 'O how many understand not the sayings of the wise; these have perished because of their foolishness, for they lacked spiritual understanding.'" This from Wikipedia.org as well, "Theobald de Hoghelande or Theobald van Hoghelande (c. 1560-1608) is an alchemist of the Renaissance, an author of several treaties of defense of the alchemy under his name, and probably under the pen name of Ewaldus Vogelius." Hoghelande is of the opinion that "the whole art is rightly to be held both difficult and dangerous, and anyone who is not improvident will eschew it as most pernicious." Alchemist Aegidius de Vadis feels the same when he says: "I shall keep silent about this science, which has led most of those who work in it into confusion, because there are few indeed who find what they seek, but an infinite number who have plunged to their ruin."

The last line in regards to thinking it another stone is referring to mistaking the Amanita muscaria for another deadly type of mushroom.

Dan Russell is helpful in explaining, "In Rome the most sacred form of an oath was (as we learn from AULUS GELLIUS), 'By Jupiter the STONE.' This, as it stands, is nonsense. But translate 'lapidem' (stone) back into the sacred tongue, or Chaldee, and the oath stands, 'By Jove, the Son,' or 'By the son of Jove.' Ben, which in Hebrew is Son, in Chaldee becomes Eben, which also signifies a stone, as may be seen in 'Eben-ezer,' 'The stone of help.' Now as the most learned inquirers into antiquity have admitted that the Roman Jovis, which was anciently the nominative, is just a form of the Hebrew Jehovah, it is evident that the oath had originally been, 'by the son of Jehovah.' This explains how the most solemn and binding oath had been taken in the form above referred to; and it shows, also, what was really meant when Bacchus, 'the son of Jovis,' was called 'the Eternal Boy.'

Saturn, 'the father of gods and men,' is Adam. Saturn destroyed all of his children by eating the forbidden fruit. Saturn, or Adam, was represented as an ill-tempered and gloomy divinity; Rhea, or Eve, exceedingly kind and gracious; and, in her benignity, she presented to her husband a stone bound in swaddling bands, which he greedily devoured, and henceforth the children of the cannibal father were safe. The stone bound in swaddling bands is, in the sacred language, 'Ebn Hatul;' but Ebn-Hat-tul also signifies 'A sin-bearing son.' It is important to note here that the forbidden fruit is represented as a stone."

Alchemist Saturninus says, "The Stone is called Adrop, that is Saturnus; because, as Saturn is the chiefest of the Planets; So our mercuriall Saturnine Stone, is the highest and most pretious of Stones."

Dan Russell further states, "The father of gods and men had destroyed his children by eating; but the reception of 'the swaddled stone' is said to have 'restored them to life' (HESIOD, Theogon.) Now, there is a great analogy between this swaddled stone that represented the "sin-bearing son," and that Olenos mentioned by Ovid, who took on him guilt not his own, and in consequence was changed into a stone. We have seen already that Olenos, when changed into a stone, was set up in Phrygia on the holy mountain of Ida. We have reason to believe that the stone which was fabled to have done so much for the children of Saturn, and was set up near the temple of Delphi, was just a representation of this same Olenos. We find that Olen was the first prophet at Delphi, who founded the first temple there (PAUSA Phocica).

As the prophets and priests generally bore the names of the gods whom they represented (Hesychius expressly tells us that the priest who represented the great god under the name of the branch in the mysteries was himself called by the name of Bacchus), this indicates one of the ancient names of the god of Delphi. If, then, there was a sacred stone on Mount Ida called the stone of Olenos, and a sacred stone in the precincts of the temple of Delphi, which Olen founded, can there be a doubt that the sacred stone of Delphi represented the same as was represented by the sacred stone of Ida? The swaddled stone set up at Delphi is expressly called by Priscian, in the place already cited, 'a god.' This god, then, that in symbol was divinely anointed, and was celebrated as having restored to life the children of Saturn, father of gods and men, as identified with the Idaean Olenos, is proved to have been regarded as occupying the very place of the Messiah, the great Sin-bearer, who came to bear the sins of men, and took their place and suffered in their room and stead; for Olenos, as we have seen, voluntarily took on him guilt of which he was personally free. While thus we have seen how much of the patriarchal faith was hid under the mystical symbols of Paganism, there is yet a circumstance to be noted in regard to the swaddled stone, that shows how the Mystery of Iniquity in Rome has contrived to import this swaddled stone of Paganism into what is called Christian symbolism. The Baitulos, or swaddled stone, was a round or globular stone.

...the cross is the chosen sign and mark of that very God whom the swaddled stone represented; and that when that God was born, it was said, 'The Lord of all the Earth is born' (WILKINSON). As the god symbolized by the swaddled stone not only restored the children of Saturn to life, but restored the lordship of the Earth to Saturn himself, which by transgression he had lost, it is not to be wondered at that it is said of 'these consecrated stones,' that while 'some were dedicated to Jupiter, and others to the sun,' 'they were considered in a more particular manner sacred to Saturn,' the Father of the gods (MAURICE), and that Rome, in consequence, has put the round stone into the hand of the image, bearing the profaned name of God the Father attached to it, and that from this source the bandaged globe, surmounted with the mark of Tammuz [the cross], has become the symbol of dominion throughout all Papal Europe."

The alchemical treatise "Clangor Buccinae" states, "The Time of every Imbibition to its Exsiccation is Twenty or Thirty natural dayes." Now I did not know what imibibition or exsiccation meant so I looked them up and imbibition is the absorption of water that results in a solid substance swelling, I would say a human being gaining excessive weight is a good example of imbibition, and exsiccation is drying out. So I would interpret that sentence as stating the life span of the mushroom is twenty to thirty days. Daustricus gives an obvious instruction as to the proper way to water your mycelium patch, "The Earth does not Germinate without frequent Irrigation, nor receive Irrigation without Dessication. Therefore at every Turn after desiccation pour Water on it temperately, neither too much, nor too little. If too much, it will be a Sea of Conturbation. If too little, all is burnt to a light Cinder."

Carl Jung says in "Alchemical Studies" on p.87, "The Turba has much to say about the fruit-bearing tree. Its fruits are of a special kind. The 'Visio Arislei' speaks of 'this most precious tree, of whose fruit he who eats shall never hunger.' The parallel to this in the Turba runs: 'I say that old man does not cease to eat of the fruits of that tree... until that old man becomes a youth.' These fruits are here equated with the bread of life in John 6: 35, but they go back beyond that to the Ethiopic Book of Enoch. (2nd cent. B.C.) Dorn calls the vessel the vas pellicanicum, and says that with its help the quinta essentia can be extracted from the prima materia. The anonymous author of the scholia to the 'Tractatus aureus Hermetis' says: 'This vessel is the true philosophical Pelican, and there is none other to be sought for in all the world.' It is the lapis itself and at the same time it contains the lapis; that is to say, the lapis itself is its own container. This formulation is borne out by the frequent comparison of the lapis to the egg or to the dragon which devours itself and gives birth to itself."

Heinrich Khunrath says, "This [the filius philosophorum], the Son of the Macrocosm, is God and creature... that [Christ], is the son of

God; the one conceived in the womb of the Macrocosm, the other in the womb of the Microcosm... Without blasphemy I say: In the Book or Mirror of Nature, the Stone of the Philosophers, the Preserver of the Macrocosm, is the symbol of Christ Jesus Crucified, Savior of the whole race of mankind, that is, of the Microcosm. From the stone you shall know in natural wise Christ, and from Christ the stone."

Carl Jung says, "In the 'Aquarium sapientum' the 'son of the great world' (filius macrocosmi, the lapis) is correlated with Christ, who is the filius microcosmi, and his blood is the quintessence, the red tincture. This is the true and authentic duplex Mercurius or Giant of twofold substance... God by nature, man, hero, etc... the triune universal essence, which is called Jehovah. The anonymous author of 'Aquarium sapientum' was not altogether clear about the triune essence; probably for good reason just as he remained anonymous.

The lapis-Christ parallel was presumably the bridge by which the mystique of the Rose entered into alchemy. This is evident first of all from the use of 'Rosarium' or 'Rosarius' (rose-gardener) as a book title. The first, as there were several, was first printed in 1550, the greater part ascribed to Arnaldus de Villanova. It seems as though the rose-coloured blood of the alchemical redeemer was derived from a rose mysticism that penetrated into alchemy, and that, in the form of the red tincture, it expressed the healing or whole-making effect of a certain kind of Eros."

The goal of the opus was to deliver the anima mundi, the world-creating spirit of God, from the chains of Physis/Nature. I feel that is a polite way of in other words stating, "absolving you of your psychosis of the ego and realizing that you are the imagination of God."

Alanus Niger says, "There are only Two fires found in the books of the Philosophers: The one dry, the other moyst: The Dry is the Elemental, the moyst is Mercury."

The red rose was also thought to be formed from the blood of Adonis, the Greek god who carried the Semetic title for Lord; this brings to mind the Rosacrucians and may perhaps be where this rose associated mysticism could have originated quite possibly. "Rose-Gardener" is a great title, just think about this for a moment. If the rose were to represent the A. muscaria since even before the days of Adonis, imagine how fitting of a title that must have been for an alchemical text.

"Mercurius, following the tradition of Hermes, is many-sided, changeable, and deceitful,' Dorn speaks of 'that incanstant Mercurius,' and 'another calls him versipellis (changing his skin, shift)... He is 'two dragons,' the 'twin,' made of 'two natures' or 'two substances... the two substances of Mercurius are thought of as dissimilar, sometimes opposed; as the dragon he is 'winged and wingless.' A parable says: 'On this mountain lies an ever-waking dragon, who is called Pantophthalmos, for he is covered with eyes on both sides of his body, before and behind, and he sleeps with some open and some closed.' There is the 'common and the philosophic' Mercurius; he consists of 'the dry and Earthy, the moist and viscous.'

He is both good and evil. The "Aurelia occulta gives a graphic description of him: I am the poison-dripping dragon, who is everywhere and can be cheaply had. That upon which I rest, and that which rests upon me, will be found within me by those who pursue their investigations in accordance with the rules of the Art. My water and fire destroy and put together; from my body you may extract the green lion and the red. But if you do not have exact knowledge of me, you will destroy your five senses with my fire. From my snout there comes a spreading poison that has brought death to many. Therefore you should skillfully separate the coarse from the fine, if you do not wish to suffer utter poverty. I bestow on you the powers of the male and the female, and also those of heaven and of Earth. The mysteries of my art must be handled with courage and greatness of mind if you would conquer me by the power of fire, for already very many have come to grief, their riches and labor lost. I am the egg of nature, known only to the wise, who in piety and modesty bring forth from me the microcosm, which was prepared for mankind by Almighty God, but given only to the few, while the many long for it in vain, that they may do good to the poor with my treasure and not fasten their souls to the perishable gold. By the philosophers I am named Mercurius; my spouse is the [philosophic] gold; I am the old dragon, found everywhere on the globe of the Earth, father and mother, young and old, very strong and very weak, death and resurrection, visible and invisible, hard and soft; I descend into the Earth and ascend to the heavens, I am the highest and the lowest, the lightest and the heaviest; often the order of nature is reversed in me, as regards colour, number, weight, and measure; I contain the light of nature; I am dark and light, I come forth from heaven and Earth; I am known and yet do not exist at all; by virtue of the sun's rays all colours shine in me, and all metals. I am the carbuncle of the sun, the most noble purified Earth, through which you may change copper, iron, tin and lead into gold." - END OF JUNG

The following passage is of a note entitled "The concept of Mercurius in Hermetic Philosophy," dated Einsiedeln, Oct 11, 1942,

discovered among Jung's papers: "...Like the Mercurius
philosophorum, the Paracelsan Mercurius is a child of Sol and Luna,
born with the help of sulphur and salt, the 'strange son of chaos,' as
Goethe calls Mephistopheles. Paracelsus names it 'omne fumosum et
humidum inquovis corpore,' the moist, breathlike or vaporous soul
dwelling in all bodies. In its highest form the Iliaster signifies the
passage of the mind or soul into another world, as took place with
Enoch, Elias, and others.' ...Paracelsan process of transforming the
Iliaster... After this discussion of some of the basic concepts of alchemy,
let us come back to the Paracelsan process of transformation. The
purpose of distillation in alchemy was to extract the volatile substance,
or spirit, from the impure body... The retorta distillatio is not a known
technical term, but presumably it meant a distillation that was in some
way turned back upon itself. It might have taken place in the vessel
called the Pelican where the distillate runs back into the belly of the
retort. This was the 'circulatory distillation,' much favored by the
alchemists. By means of the 'thousandfold distillation' they hoped to
achieve a particularly 'refined' result... The fire used was a symbolical
fire, and the distillation had to start 'from the midst of the center'(ex
medio centri)... The accentuation of the center is again a fundamental
idea in alchemy."

The title of the process itself indicates that the Iliaster is the
Amanita muscaria, transforming the lead into gold is often used as a
way to deter those who would use the knowledge to profit, as the
mushroom is poisonous when wet due to the ibotenic acid, it is as
useless as lead unless processed with the special alchemical knowledge
that can turn the lead into precious spiritual alchemical gold. Here the

author obviously describes an extremely potent extraction method. Alchemy or the secret shamanic wisdom of preparing the deity, and figuring out how to get extremely potent dosages, was indeed the precursor to our modern day chemistry.

Nine Greek Lives

 Plutarch

 (Selections whole and in part)

"Theseus, the founder of the lovely and famed city of Athens; on his father's side he traces his descent from Erechtheus and the earliest inhabitants of Attica and on his mother's from Pelops. Pelops was the most powerful of the kings in the Peloponnese, not so much by virtue of his wealth as of the number of his children. He married many of his daughters to the highest in the land and established many of his sons far and wide as rulers of the Peloponnesian cities. One of these, named Pittheus, was the grandfather of Theseus and founded the city of Troezen; this is, in fact, only a small city, but he himself had the reputation of being the wisest of men and the most deeply versed in the lore of his age. Pittheus is a masculine form of Pitthea ("pine-goddess"), worshipped in autumn when Attis-Adonis was sacrificed on his pine.

Theseus admired Heracles above all other heroes, and liked nothing better than to listen to anyone who could speak of the kind man he was, and especially to people who had been witnesses of anything he had said or done. In fact he was evidently passing through the same state of mind that Themistocles experienced many generations later, when he said that he could not sleep for thinking of Miltiades' victory. So with Theseus the valour of Heracles became his dream by night and in the daytime his desire to emulate the hero seized hold of him and spurred him on to achieve such exploits himself.

As it happen, the two were the sons of first cousins, and so related to one another. Aethra was the daughter of Pittheus, while Heracles' mother Alcmene, was the daughter of Lysidice, and Lysidice and Pittheus were brother and sister, their parents being Pelops and Hippodameia. Historians say that the two heroes often met, and that it was at Theseus' desire that Heracles was initiated into the Eleusinian Mysteries and was also purified before the initiation at his own request, on account of various headstrong actions he had committed. It was at Eleusis ('advent'), a Mycenaean city, that the great Eleusinian Mysteries were celebrated, in the month called Boedromion ('running for help').

The story of Hecale, too, who is said to have welcomed and entertained Theseus on this expedition, seems to have some truth in it. The people of the demes in that neighbourhood were in the habit of meeting to perform the Hecalesian rites in honour of Zeus Hecalus, and they also paid honours to Hecale, whom they called by the diminutive name of Hecaline. This was because when she entertained Theseus, she caressed him as elderly people do children and called him affectionately by diminutive names in the same way, even though he was quite a young man.

In Athens there was a great plague and all the rivers dried up. Apollo then declared to them that if they placated Minos and became reconciled with him, the wrath of heaven would cease and they would be delivered from their sufferings. Thereupon they sent heralds and appealed to Minos and entered into an agreement to send him a tribute every nine years, consisting of seven young men and seven girls.

According to the most dramatic version of the story, when these young men and women reached Crete, they were thrown into the Labyrinth and there killed by the Minotaur, or else wandered about and finally perished because they could find no way out; while the Minotaur itself, as Euripes tells us, was .A mingled form, where two strange shapes combined And different natures, man and bull, were joined..."

This bull and man business, has to do with mushrooms. They make the man feel like a bull wanting to press his crown against objects that provide resistance. Theseus' s killing of the bull-headed Asterius, called the Minotaur, or 'Bull of Minos'; his wrestling match with Taurus; and his capture of the Cretan bull, are all versions of the same event. It was in bull form that the king seems to have coupled ritually with the Chief-priestess as Moon-cow; you must remember this last sentence.

I believe this is from Herodotus: The nearest any man had come to coupling with Athena was when her brother Hephaestus, the crippled blacksmith of the gods, whose talents of craftsmanship were as limitless as his bandy legs were weak, had been so overcome with desire for his sister that he had hobbled after her, sweaty and soot-stained, and sought to take her in his arms. Athena, with icy contempt, had brushed him aside- but not before Hephaestus, shuddering with excitement, had ejaculated all over her thigh. Wiping the mess off with a tangle of wool, the goddess had then dropped it, still sodden, down onto Attica- where the semen, like heavy dew, had moistened the womb of Mother Earth. From the fertilizing of "the grain-growing fields" had been born a child with the coiled tail of a snake. Athena, adopting him, had named him Erechtheus. She had settled him on the Acropolis, "in her own wealthy temple," and there, "to this day, with each revolving year, the sons of Athens offer him bulls and rams."

The Greeks and Their Gods
 By W.K.C. Guthrie

"The fullest account of the oracle of Trophonios at Lebadeia is that of Pausanias, and we have his word that it is that of an eyewitness, for Pausanias claims to have consulted Trophonios himself and gone through all the hair-raising experiences which such consultation involved. We may feel fairly confident that the procedure had not changed since the days of Euripides Aristophanes; it is therefore worth setting out in full.

As to the oracle, the procedure is as follows. When a man decides to go down to visit Trophonios, he is first of all lodged in a certain building for an appointed number of days, this being sacred to the Daimonos Agathon (Good Daimon) and to Tykhe (Fortune). While he lodges there, among other regulations for purity he abstains from hot baths, bathing only in the river Herkyna. Meat he has in plenty from the sacrifices, for he who descends sacrifices to Trophonios himself and to the children of Trophonios, to Apollon also and Kronos, to Zeus surnamed King, to Hera Charioteer, and to Demeter whom they surname Europa and say was the nurse of Trophonios. At each sacrifice a diviner is present, who looks into the entrails of the victim, and after an inspection prophesies to the person descending whether Trophonios will give him a kind and gracious reception. The entrails of the other victims do not declare the mind of Trophonios as much as a ram, which each inquirer sacrifices over a pit on the night he descends, calling upon

Agamedes. Even though the previous sacrifices have appeared propitious, no account is taken of them unless the entrails of this ram indicate the same; but if they agree, then the inquirer descends in good hope.

The procedure of the descent is this. First, during the night he is taken to the river Herkyna by two boys of the citizens about thirteen years old, named Hermai, who after taking him there anoint him with oil and wash him. It is these who wash the descender, and do all the other necessary services as his attendant boys. After this he is taken by the priests, not at once to the oracle, but to fountains of water very near to each other. Here he must drink water called the water of Lethe, that he may forget all that he has been thinking of hitherto, and afterwards he drinks of another water, the water of Mnemosyne (Memory), which causes him to remember what he sees after his descent. After looking at the image which they say was made by Daidalos (it is not shown by the priests save to such as are going to visit Trophonios), having seen it, worshipped it and prayed, he proceeds to the oracle, dressed in a linen tunic, with ribbons girding it, and wearing the boots of the country.

The oracle is on the mountain, beyond the grove. Round it is a circular basement of white marble, the circumference of which is about that of the smallest threshing-floor, while its height is just short of two cubits. On the basement stand spikes, which, like the cross-bars holding them together, are of bronze, while through them has been made a double door. Within the enclosure is a chasm in the Earth, not natural, but artificially constructed after the most accurate masonry. The shape of this structure is like that of a bread-oven. Its breadth across is the middle one might conjecture to be about four cubits, and its depth also could not be estimated to extend to more than eight cubits. They have made no way of descent to the bottom, but when a man comes to Trophonios, they bring him a narrow, light ladder. (I want to know if Jacob let him borrow it, or if he stole it.) After going down he finds a hole between the floor and the structure. Its breadth appeared to be two spans, and its height one span. The descender lies with his back on the ground, holding barley-cakes kneaded with honey, thrusts his feet into the hold and himself follows, trying hard to get his knees into the hole. After his knees the rest of his body is at once swiftly drawn in, just as the largest and most rapid river will catch a man in its eddy and carry him under. After this those who have entered the shrine learn the future, not in one and the same way in all cases, but by sight sometimes and at other times by hearing. The return upwards is by the same mouth, the feet darting out first.

They say that no one who has made the descent has been killed, save only one of the bodyguard of Demetrios. But they declare that he performed none of the usual rites in the sanctuary, and he descended not to consult the god but in the hope of stealing gold and silver from the shrine. It is said the body of this man appeared in a different place, and was not cast out at the sacred mouth . . . After his ascent from Trophonios the inquirer is again taken in hand by the priests, who set him upon a chair called the chair of Mnemosyne (Memory), which stands not far from the shrine, and they ask of him, when seated there, all he has seen or learned. After gaining this information they then entrust him to his relatives. These lift him, paralysed with terror and unconscious both of himself and of his surroundings, and carry him to the building where he lodged before with Tykhe (Fortune) and the

Daimon Agathos (Good Spirit). Afterwards, however, he will recover all his faculties, and the power to laugh will return to him. What I write is not hearsay; I have myself inquired of Trophonios and seen other inquirers. Those who have descended into the shrine of Trophonios are obliged to dedicate a tablet on which is written all that each has heard or seen...

In Celtic myth the labyrinth came to mean the royal tomb; and that it also did so among the early Greeks is suggested by its definition in the Etymologicum Magnum as 'a mountain cave', and by Eustathius (On Homer's Odyssey xi. p. 1688) as 'a subterranean cave'. To escape from the labyrinth, therefore, is to be reincarnate. We may notice the observance of a preliminary regimen designed as it is of the preparations for an invocation of Hekate described by Apollonius Rhodius. Pausanias also vividly describes the effects of the fright, although he adds from his personal experience that the power of laughter does return after some time. The honey-cakes are to pacify the serpents, which we know from other accounts to have been encountered by the visitor as he entered the adyton. Aristophanes in the Clouds makes Strepsiades exclaim, before entering the school of Socrates, "Give me a honey-cake first, for I am as frightened at going in as if it were the cave of Trophonios!" Guthrie, author of 'The Greeks and Their Gods', has noticed two divisions of prophecy- "sane" prophecy or omen-reading and mad or inspired prophecy involving actual possession by the god. The underground sanctuary of Trophonios was a manteion, and where this sort of prophecy is practised, it will usually be found that an Earth-spirit is at the bottom of it. Gaia, the Earth herself, was "the first of prophets".

Below is an excerpt from an online blog-turned-book.

"Trophonios and his brother Agamedes were architects, and built the first temple to Apollon at Delphi. One story says that they stole gold from a client, who set a trap for them which caught Agamedes, and Trophonios cut off his brother's head so he couldn't be identified; at which act the Earth opened up and swallowed him. Another story says Apollon himself killed the brothers after they built His temple, so that they would always be remembered for it. In either case, awhile later, during a drought in Boiotia, the locals sent envoys to Delphi to ask for a cure; the oracle told them to consult Trophonios at Lebadeia. They could not find the oracle, until one of the envoys was inspired to follow a swarm of bees on their way – they flew into a hole in the ground, and that's where he found the oracle. He was said to have been taught from Trophonios directly what the customs and rites there should be.

Thereafter it became a respected oracular center. However, unlike most of the large oracles of Greece, where a prophet would speak on behalf of the god (like at Delphi, or Claros) or interpret signs from the god (like at Dodona), at Lebadeia the person seeking an oracle would descend into Trophonios' cave themselves and consult the god directly. The procedure was quite lengthy, but fortunately we know most of the details due to the reporting of Pausanias, who consulted the oracle himself.

First, the querent would stay in a building at the site for several days. While there, he would have to bathe in the cold river Herkyna, taking no hot baths. He would sacrifice to a slew of gods, including Trophonios, Apollon, Kronos, Zeus, Hera and Demeter (and also eat some of the meat from those sacrifices). Each time, diviners would interpret the entrails of the animals to decide whether Trophonios would grant him an audience.

If all went well with the sacrifices, on the final night he would be washed in the river and anointed with oil. He would then be taken to two fountains called Lethe and Mnemosyne (Forgetting and Memory, two legendary rivers of the underworld). He would drink the first in order to forget all that was in his mind before, and the second to remember what he would see below. He would then worship at a secret statue said to have been made by Daidalos. Dressed in a linen garment with ribbons, and wearing locally made shoes, he would be led to the entrance of the oracle. Descending down a ladder, he would reach a stopping point with an even smaller hole. Holding two honeyed barley cakes as offerings (probably to the sacred snakes), he would put himself feet first into the hole, and get sucked down into the chasm.

Within the cave, he would receive the answer he was looking for, sometimes by visions, sometimes by things heard. Then he would return to the world above feet first again. The priests would sit him upon the Chair of Memory and ask him what he learned, which was then written on a tablet and kept in the shrine. The experience was said to be so terrifying and traumatic that the querent would be paralyzed in a sort of trance, and afterwards unable to laugh for quite some time, though eventually he would return to his normal self. However, this did not seem to deter many people from seeking the advice of Trophonios.

We know very little about what actually happened down in the chasm. Of course, many people will say that it was a theatrical performance of the priests, who would manufacture "visions" for gullible querents. But I do not hold such a poor view of the ancient

Greeks, and I believe that when oracles maintain solid reputations for centuries, it is because a god or daimon is involved. Plutarch relates a story about Timarchus descending to consult Trophonios: he lies down in the darkness but cannot tell if he is asleep or awake; he feels something like a blow to his head which releases his soul to have visions and hear voices; he feels another pain in his head and passes out, only to come to almost two days later, returning to describe the many wonders he witnessed."

Chapter Two: This Christ Gushed Forth

Justin Martyr says: "As a fount of living water from God... this Christ gushed forth!"

"The Histories" -by Herodotus Book II; p. 123 states, "This pinecone staff is a symbol of the solar god Osiris, Egyptian Museum, Turino, Italy. Osiris originated in Egypt, where he was their Messiah, who died for the good of his people, and whose Mother, Isis, was worshipped as the Virgin Mother. Herodotus notes, "The inhabitants of a big city in Ethiopia named Meroe, said to be the capital, worship Zeus and Dionysus(Osiris) alone of the gods, holding them in great honor." Plutarch translates the name Isis to mean wisdom. Plutarch further asserts that the Greeks recognized in Osiris the same person whom they revered under the names of Dionysos and Bacchus(opposite).

This is what the 'Father of History' 4th Century BC historian Herodotus has to say of Dionysus: "Not all Egyptians worship the same gods - the only two to be universally worshipped are Isis and Osiris, who, they say, is Dionysus. The Egyptians say that Apollo and Artemis are the children of Isis and Dionysus, and that Leto saved them and brought them up. In Egypt Apollo is Horus and Demeter is Isis."

(Image: Bacchus)

Dionysus, the Greek god, also carries a pinecone staff as a fertility symbol, perhaps this correlates with the fact that Osiris had a pinecone staff.

The Magnum Opus or The Great Work by Albert Pike states, "The mysteries of Venus and Adonis belonged principally to Syria and Phoenicia, whence they passed into Greece and Sicily. Venus, Easter, or Astarte was the Great Female Deity of the Phoenicians, as Hercules, Melkarth or Adoni was their Cheif God."

Michael R. Aldrich regarding his obtainment of Wasson's help, "...What caught my attention was Euripides' account (Bacchae lines 13-22) of the route Dionysus took to and from India: through Lydia and Phrygia across Persia to Bactria (Afghanistan), then returning through Medea, Arabia Felix and Asia Minor to Thebes. Intoxication cults had existed in each of these places, and Euripides was, in effect, outlining a network of psychoactive drug religions in the ancient Middle East. Most of them involved the use of alcohol, but some were more mysterious. What, for instance, was the Soma of ancient India, recorded in the Vedas? It was not alcohol (surya) or cannabis (bhang), for both are distinguished from Soma in the Rg Vedas... that Soma was the fly-agaric mushroom... that the worshippers of Dionysus added Amanita muscaria to their wine for the hallucinogenic frenzy Euripides depicts in the Bacchae."

"The original Greek words for 'to be drunk' and 'to make drunk' are methyein and methyskein.

"Before he had advanced to agriculture he had a drink made of naturally fermented honey, the drink we now know as mead, which the Greeks called methy or methe. This mead made of honey appears in

ancient legends. When Zeus would intoxicate Kronos (Saturn) he gave
him not wine, Porphyry says, for wine did not exist, but a honey-drink
to darken his senses. Night says to Zeus: 'When prostrate beneath the
lofty oaks you find him, lie drunken with the work of murmuring bees,
then bind him.' Plato tells us how when Poros falls asleep in the garden
of Zeus he is drunk not with wine but with nectar, for wine was not yet.
Nectar, the ancient drink of the gods, is mead made with honey; and
men know this for they offer to the primitive Earth-god libations of
honey. Plutarch says mead (methy/methe) was used as a libation before
the appearance of the vine, and even now those of the barbarians who
do not drink wine drink honey-drink (meliteion)." Zeus's nectar was
described as a super natural red wine."

        - Shamanism and Drug Propaganda The Patriarchy and the
Drug War, Dan Russell

        When reading 'Ancient Persia,' by Josef Wiesehofer, I learned
while Soviet excavators were digging at Nisa, at a city ruins from
Parthia (modern day Iran), "The excavators and art experts were
particularly impressed by the more than 50 ivory rhytons (horn-shaped
drinking vessels with a figure at their narrow end), which, due to their
weight, must have been used only on ritual or ceremonial occasions.
Both the 'classical pieces' with figures of centaurs and an Aphrodite, the
'Oriental' ones ending in griffins, display friezes with Dionysiac scenes
and the twelve Olympic gods..."

        Tammuz is later associated with Bacchus; The Roman god of
wine and intoxication, equated with the Greek Dionysus. The old-Italian
god of fertility and growth in nature. In later times Liber ("the free
one") was equated with Dionysus and became thus a god of viniculture.

His feminine counterpart is Libera. Their festival, the Liberia, was observed on March 17th, keep in mind the four leaf clover and St. Patrick's Day which is also celebrated on March 17th.

Ovid said that Dionysos invented honey, interestingly enough, ancient Egypt ruins are often found to contain honey, some still edible, in fact honey was used as a preservative because of its natural long lasting qualities. Often mushroom caps were stored in honey pots for long periods of time when the demand for mushrooms outweighed the supply in seasonal times, which required for the saving up of mushrooms from previous seasons. Mushrooms would rot if it were not for the storing of the dried caps in honey jars. The next picture is of the Assyrian winged god with a pinecone, representing power of regeneration. Traceable to Tammuz of Babylon.

Since the ultimate goal of religion is the securing of eternal life, we should not be surprised that the Pope should be carrying the ultimate Pagan symbol of eternal life. This is typical in Roman Catholic services and ornaments. Most Paganism in history is traceable directly back to Tammuz of Babylon. His mother, Semiramis, was the first Virgin Mother in world history, predating the birth of Jesus Christ by over a thousand years. Did you know that the Roman Catholic practice of making the Sign of the Cross originated in Babylon as people paid homage to their Messiah, Tammuz, who "died for the good of his people". People would constantly publicly demonstrate their love and adoration for Tammuz by making the sign of the cross.

The largest pinecone in the world is at Vatican Square in the 'Court of the Pinecone'. Pagans revere the Evergreen because it symbolizes Eternal Life to them. They further revere the "fruit" of the Evergreen, the pinecone. The Amanita muscaria happens to grow underneath Evergreen trees due to the fact that the mycelium feeds off of the organic matter that falls from the tree, the pinecone thus being the symbolic fruit just as the Mushroom is the fruit of the secret unseen magical powers of the tree.

The 'Expository Dictionary of New Testament Words', says the cross originated among the Babylonians of ancient Chaldea, used as a symbol of the god Tammuz.

"Almost any book of ancient Egypt shows the use of the Tau cross (shaped like the letter .T.) on old monuments and walls of ancient temples." – Russell

This is the court of the pinecone.

"The bronze hand, top, dates from the late Roman Empire, when all forms of divination from scrying to astrology, flourished. The hand bears the symbols, such as a cockerel's head and a pinecone, of the Roman mystery cult of Dionysus. Worshippers of Dionysus would work themselves into a frenzy, in which they might see visions of the future."
- Wikipedia

Seymour says that the cross, unchanged for thousands of years, "was reverenced... among the Chaldeans, Phoenicians, Mexicans, and every ancient people of both hemispheres,. The Cross in Tradition,

History, and Art, pp. 22, 26. The cross had been a sacred symbol of India for centuries among non-Christians. Prescott reports that when the Spaniards first landed in Mexico, they were shocked to behold the cross, sacred emblem of their own Catholic faith, reverenced in Aztec temples. A heathen temple in Palenque, Mexico, founded in the ninth century B.C., was known as .The Temple of the Cross.. Ancient Mexicans worshipped a cross as tota (our father), similar to apostate Israelites who worshipped a piece a wood as "my father," Jeremiah 2:27. In 46 B.C., Roman coins show Jupiter holding a long scepter terminating in a cross.

While uncovering this truth, I uncovered many others, mainly that Saturnalia was most likely involving the red Amanita muscaria mushroom, and the fact that the number twenty-two is the Chaldean symbol which equates to a cross when Jesus would more likely have been impaled on a T shaped crucifix leads me to believe that there is a connection between the number being at the top of the Hebrew Kabbalah and Tammuz being the Amanita muscaria. I am blatantly trying to say that the Amanita muscaria, or Adam is the most important entheogen to ancient Hebrew shamans which is why it is at the top of the Kabbalah, and that the corresponding twenty-one elements may perhaps be the most sacred plants to their culture.

Adam is known as the Roman Bacchus, the Greek Dionysus, the Phoenician/Babylonian Thammuz, the Egyptian Osiris; all whom were gods of intoxication, all of whom were sacrificed, descended to hell, brought back to life, and celebrated, and all of whom were celebrated for the purpose of "purification of souls"(Servius). The expression used in Exodus 28:38, for "bearing iniquity" or sin in a vicarious manner is "nsha eon" (the first letter eon being ayn). A synonym for eon, "iniquity," is aon (the first letter being aleph). In Chaldee the first letter a becomes i, and therefore aon, "iniquity," is ion. Then nsha "to bear," in the participle active is "nusha." As the Greeks had no sh, that became nusa. De, or Da, is the demonstrative pronoun signifying "That" or "The great." And thus "D'ion-nusa" is exactly "The great sin-bearer."

"Now, this Babylonian god, known in Greece as "The sin-bearer," and in India as the "Victim-Man," among the Buddhists of the East, the original elements of whose system are clearly Babylonian, was commonly addressed as the "Saviour of the world." The true Messiah was prophesied of under the title of the "Man whose name was the branch," he was celebrated not only as the "Branch of Cush," but as the "Branch of God," graciously given to the Earth for healing all the ills that flesh is heir to. He was worshipped in Babylon under the name of El-Bar, or "God the Son." Under this very name he is introduced by Berosus, the Chaldean historian, as the second in the list of Babylonian sovereigns. In Pagan Rome itself, as Ovid testifies, he was worshipped under the name of the "Eternal Boy." - The Deification of the Child

Adam is the "red one", the "red man", the "first man"; Adon was the title for Thammuz, the young spouse and lover of Ishtar, the Babylonian Earth mother goddess. He was a god who died annually to be reborn each spring. He was mourned by the women of the Near East during the month of July when they would sit in the streets and wail for their beloved lost god. The symbolism of the Greek myth shows that each winter Thammuz/Adonis/Adam died and the whole Earth died with him; each spring he rose again and the whole world came into resurrection. Spring rites in the Near East were dedicated to Istar, the spouse of Thammuz. The pagan rites carried over into Christian Easter.

The myth of Hylas 'of the woodland', Adonis, Lityerses, and Linus describes the annual mourning for the sacred king, or his boy-surrogate, sacrificed to placate the goddess of vegetation. This same surrogate, sacrificed to placate Triptolemus, who rode in a serpent-drawn chariot and carried sacks of corn, to symbolize that his death brought wealth. A primitive taboo rested on red-coloured food, which might be offered to the dead only; and the pomegranate was supposed to have sprung from the blood of Adonis, or Tammuz.

The association of the Adamic name with a red or purple colour came down to modern times by paths other than Hebrew or Phoenician traditions. The name saw phonetic changes as the IE "Don" went to "Dom = dam," but different applications. The word purple comes from the Greek porphyra which comes from the Latin purpura, "in early use meaning crimson." The Roman Catholic Church inherited the ancient tradition of royal colors from pagan Roman nobility; Bishops and Cardinals still retain those colors in both crimson and purple robes.

These traditions all reflect a very ancient practice of distinguishing the mark of royal inheritance and regal right said to be all from the Red One, or Adom. Biblical scholars generally accept the name Adom to mean "red." In western Bible-thumpers eyes it refers to "the flush of the white complexion." Most agree that this is a later imaginary interpretation and that the real history is simply lost. I disagree, I believe adom refers to the red color found in the Amanita muscaria.

"Our races, all cosmogonies show, have sprung from divine

races, by whatever name they are called. The Chaldeans had their ten and seven Anedots, which was the generic name for their Dragons of Wisdom. The name of the Dragon in Chaldea was not written phonetically, but was represented by two monograms, probably meaning, according to the Orientalists, "the scaly one." We find the priests assuming the names of the gods they served, the "Dragons" held throughout all antiquity as the symbols of Immortality and Wisdom, of secret Knowledge and of Eternity. The allegory of Oannes, the Anedot, reminds us of the Dragon and Snake-Kings; the Nagas who in Buddhist legends instruct people in wisdom on lakes and rivers, and end by becoming converts to the good Law and Arhats. Musarus Oannes, the Anedot, known in the Chaldean "legend," transmitted through Berosus and other ancient writers as Dagon, the "Man-Fish," came to the early Babylonians as a reformer and an instructor. Appearing from the Erythraean (Red) Sea, he brought them civilization, letters and sciences, law, astronomy, religion, teaching them agriculture, geometry, and the arts in general. There were Anedoti who came after him; but Musarus Oannes was "the first to appear, and this he did in the reign of Ammenon, the third of the ten antediluvian Kings whose (divine) Dynasty ended with Xisuthrus, the Chaldean Noah." The meaning of the allegory is evident. The "fish" is an old and very suggestive symbol of the Mystery-language, as is also "water;" Hea was the god of the sea and Wisdom, and the sea serpent was one of his emblems, his priests being "serpents" or Initiates. The hidden meaning becomes clear to the Occultist once he is told that "this being (Oannes) was accustomed to pass the day among men, teaching; and when the sun had set, he retired again into the sea, passing the night in the deep, for he was amphibios," i.e., he belonged to two planes, the spiritual and the physical. ... Oannes is dimly reflected in Jonah, and even in John the Precursor, both connected with Fish and Water. Layard showed long ago that the "fish's head" was simply a head gear, the mitre worn by priests and gods, made in the form of a fish's head, and which in a very little modified form is what we see even now on the heads of the high Lamas and Romish Bishops. Osiris had such a mitre. The fish's tail is simply the train of a long stiff mantle as depicted on some Assyrian tablets, the form being seen reproduced in the sacerdotal gold cloth garment worn during service by the modern Greek priests." -Helena Blavatsky

Edom is actually a form of adom. According to the story in Gen 25:29-34 Isaac's eldest twin son Esau picked up the nickname Edom, meaning red, because he was famished from hunting in the field and wanted the red (adom) stew his younger twin brother Jacob was making. For this favor Jacob (Israel) demanded his older brother's birthright. Jacob later became the father of the Hebrew tribes. Edom is actually the name Adom with a very slight change in the vowel sound.

Chapter Three: Cows are Holy

Dan Russell sheds much light on the ancient lunar and bovine cults so dominant in our past... *"Evidence indicates that the indigenous peoples of Seir-Edom, the Shasu, the forerunners of the Edomites of the Bible, may hold the key to explaining the development of the Israelite race around the end of the Late Bronze Age. They would appear to have been the original worshippers of Yahweh, who was primarily a mountain god with bovine and lunar qualities. It seems like they were a tribal confederacy brought together by a core of Egyptian individuals, former priests and followers of the Aten."..."Also they found many coins, written on them was '[Coin of] the king of kings Arsaces, the beneficent, just, excellence [excellent ruler] and friend of the Greeks.' "Obviously Greek influence was very strong for one reason or another. In 206 B.C. another very prominent deity was imported into Rome from Phrygia: The mother-goddess Cybele, which used to be worshipped right next to Dionysus. Her orgiastic rites were very similar and the high priests were castrated, told to live as women, performed animal blood sacrifices, bathed in blood, and cut themselves open during certain ceremonies."* -End of Russell

"The erection of statues, temples, and altars is not an accepted practice amongst them, and anyone who does such a thing is considered a fool, because, presumably, the Persian religion is not anthropomorphic like the Greek. Zeus, in their system, is the whole circle of the heavens, and they sacrifice to him from the tops of mountains... They learned from the Assyrians and Arabians the cult of Uranian Aphrodite. The Assyrian name from Aphrodite is Mylitta, Arabian Alilat, the Persian Mitra." -Herodotus

"The Historical epics are probably the most complex sources for a Mesopotamian historian. We have at our disposal a number of texts in the Akkadian language, which have known historical figures as their main character. Yet, some of the tales about these men have clear mythological contents, such as the story of Gilgamesh's fight with the bull of heaven. So how are we to evaluate such stories, except by deciding what seems humanly possible (a battle with Kish) and what seems impossible (a fight against the bull of heaven)?" -Cuneiform Texts and the Writing of History by Marc Van De Mieroop

"The principal deity of the Edomites was Qos, or Quash, pronounced cow-us… an Aramaic inscription on a horned Edomite stela found near Petra refers to Qos-Allah, or "Qos is God", while a carved stone scarab found by Crystal M Bennett at an Edomite site named Tawilan… is thought to be an abstract representation of Qaush as the moon god… it shows a star within a crescent on top of a pillar… thus we can see that there appears to be a direct line of transmission between Yahweh, the god of the Shasu, and Israelites, Qaush, the god of the Iron Age Edomites, and Dhushara, the high god of the Nabateans. All of them seem to have been connected with the moon, bulls, pillars and high mountains… Shara, the mountain abode of Dhushara, is a later form of Seir… This we can see from the fact that the Aramaean Shara is phonetically the same as the Mandaean word Sera, or Sira, meaning "the moon"… Mandaean script derives from a Nabataean original, confirming that "Shara" and, as we have already seen, Seir mean, simply, "moon", or "of the moon"."
-Tutankhamun – The Exodus Conspiracy Pg 219

Obviously the moon was used as a calendar but its association with water is also very important here. Mushrooms are ninety-percent water, not to mention the plethora of water association to be found in alchemy. In ancient times the moon was considered to be the oldest of the planets, preceding the Sun, as day follows night. The moon was seen to control the cycles of nature, causing grass, trees, and crops to grow. It increased the yield of flocks and herds, and was responsible for childbirth among the human race. In ancient Babylon, modern-day Iraq, the moon was worshipped under the name Sin, from the Sumerian en-zu, or zu-en, meaning 'the lord of knowledge'. Jordan Maxwell enlightened me to the fact that the usage of the letter u usually denotes a connection with water.

Pashupati (Sanskrit: Pasupati), "Lord of cattle", is an epithet of the Hindu deity Shiva. In Vedic times it was used as an epithet of Rudra. By the time the ancient Sanskrit epic The Ramayana was written, the name Rudra was taken as a synonym for Shiva and the two names are used interchangeably. One could say without argument that the "Lord of cattle" was Rudra, the "brilliant, fierce, red one, from the earth."

The Argives worshipped the moon as a cow, because the horned new moon was regarded as the source of all water, and therefore of cattle fodder. Her three colors: white for the new moon, red for the harvest moon, black for the moon when it waned, represented the three ages of the Moon-goddess – Maiden, Nymph, and Crone.

The story of Inachus's sons and their search for Io the moon-cow has influenced that of Agenor's sons and their search for Europe. Phoenix in a masculine form of Pheonissa ('the red one'), a title given to the moon as goddess of Death-in-life. Europe means 'broad-face', a synonym for the full moon, and a title of the Moon-goddesses Demeter at Lebadia and Astarte at Sidon.

Nemesis was the Moon-goddess as Nymph and, in the earliest form of the love-chase myth, she pursued the sacred king through his seasonal changes of hare, fish, bee, mouse, and finally devoured him. With the victory of the patriarchal system, the chase was reversed: the goddess now fled from Zeus.

Eumolpus represents the singing shepherds who brought in the child; Triptolemus is a cowherd, in service to Io the Moon-goddess as cow. It seems that late in the second millennium B.C. the sea-faring Aeolians, who had agreed to worship the pre-Hellenic Moon-goddess as their divine ancestress and protectress, became tributary to the Zeus-worshipping Achaeans, and were forced to accept the Olympian religion. But in Crete, the ancient mystical tradition that Zeus was born and died annually lingered on. Crete itself is a Greek word meaning "Ruling Goddess" derived from crateia. The myth of Zagreus concerns the annual sacrifice of a boy, which took place in ancient Crete: a surrogate for Minos the Bull-king. He reigned for a single day, went through a dance illustrative of the five seasons and then was eaten raw.

White, red, and black, the colours of Minos's heifer, were also those of Io the Moon-cow; those of Augeias's sacred bulls; and on a Cretan vase those of the Minos bull which carried off Europe. Moreover, clay or plaster tripods sacred to the Cretan goddess found at Ninou Khani, and a similar tripod found at Mycenae, were painted in white, red, and black and according to Ctesias's Indica, these were the colors of the unicorn's horn – the unicorn, as a calendar symbol represented the Moon-goddess's dominion over the five seasons of the

Osirian year. Minos seems to have been the royal title of a Hellenic dynasty which ruled Crete early in the second millennium, each king ritually marrying the Moon-priestess of Cnossus and taking his title of "Moon-being" from her.

The filthy demons called Empusae, children of Hecate, disguise themselves in the forms of bitches, cows, or beautiful maidens and, in the latter shape, will lie with men by night, sucking their vital forces until they die. The Empusae ('forcers-in') are greedily seductive female demons, a concept probably brought to Greece from Palestine, where they went by the name of Lilim ('children of Lilith'). Lilith ('scritch-owl') was a Canaanite Hecate, and the Jews made amulets to protect themselves against her as late as the Middle Ages. They could change themselves into beautiful maidens or cows, as well as bitches, because the Bitch Hecate, being a member of the Moon-triad, was the same goddess as Aphrodite, or cow-eyed Hera.

Perhaps the most striking find extending through all four levels of the ruins was a series of large globular "owl vases," with handles like upraised arms or wings rising from the shoulder. Eyes and nose were modeled on the neck; and female breasts, navel and vulva were often shown on the body of the vessel. Schliemann regarded these interesting objects as representations of Athena, the protecting goddess of Homer's Troy. He was sure the scholars were wrong in translating glaukopis as "gray-eyed" or "bright-eyed"; it must rather mean "owl-eyed," since glaux is the classical Greek work for "owl" and the owl was Athena's bird. He also notes the discovery of many terra-cotta "idols of Hera, more or less broken, in the form of a woman or in that of a cow". As with the Trojan "owl-eyed Athena," he immediately recognized in these little figures a connection with a Homeric deity, in this case Hera bo-opis ("ox-eyed").

Ixion's name, formed from ischys ("strength") and io ("moon"), also suggests ixias ("mistletoe"). As an oak-king with mistletoe genitals, representing the thunder-god, he ritually married the rain-making Moon-goddess. The Moon-goddess of the oak-cult was known as Dia ("of the sky"), a title of the Dodonan Oak-goddess and therefore Zeus's wife Hera. On an Etruscan mirror, Ixion is shown spread-eagled to a fire-wheel, with mushroom tinder at his feet; elsewhere, he is bound in the same "fivefold bond" with which the Irish hero Curoi tied Cuchulain – bent backwards into a hoop, with his wrists, ankles, and neck tied together, like Osiris in the Book of the Dead.

"Sisyphus", though the Greeks understood it to mean 'very wise', is spelt Sesephus by Hesychius, and is thought to be a Greek variant of Tesup, the Hittite Sun-God, identical with Atabyrius the Sun-god of Rhodes, whose sacred animal was a bull. Sisyphus's 'shameless stone' was originally a sun disk, and the hill up which he rolled it is the vault of Heaven. Moreover, Sisyphus is invariably placed next to Ixion in Tartarus, and Ixion's fire-wheel is the symbol of the sun. This explains why the people of Ephyra sprang from mushrooms-mushrooms were the ritual tinder of Ixion's fire-wheel, and the Sun-god demanded human burnt sacrifices to inaugurate his year.

With a new caution he (Schliemann) says of the so called Aryan motifs on the spindle whorls, "I abstain from discussing whether this ornamentation may by symbolical or not..." Similarly, in describing some little bird-faced statuettes, he hedges slightly compared with his previous confident identifications of the owl vases with Athena. "As all these rude figures represent the same form, there can be no doubt that they are idols of a female goddess, the patron deity of the place, whether she may have been called Ate, or Athene, or have had any other name..." But he still cannot resist the urge to tie in his finds with mythology and adds: "There appears to be the highest probability that all of them are copies of the celebrated primeval Palladium [image of Pallas Athene], to which was attached the fate of Troy, and which was fabled to have fallen from heaven. Zeus's rape of Europe, which records an early Hellenic occupation of Crete, has been deduced from pre-Hellenic pictures of the Moon-priestess triumphantly riding on the Sun-bull, her victim; the scene survives in eight moulded plaques of blue glass, found in the Mycenaean city of Midea. Zeus's rapes apparently refer to Hellenic conquests of the goddess's ancient shrines, such as that on Mount Cyllene; his marriages, to an ancient custom of giving the title "Zeus" to the sacred king of the oak cult. Hermes, his son by the rape of Maia – title of the Earth-goddess as Crone – was originally not a god, but the totemistic virtue of a phallic pillar, or cairn. Such pillars were the center of an orgiastic dance in the goddess's honour. Laboratory analyses of thirteen stone axes, or celts, from the lowest level showed that they were of jade, one of them a rare white variety, which must have been imported in rough or finished form from very distant eastern sources. Pure copper, not bronze, was the basic metal, and the art of gilding was known. "We, therefore, find in use among these primitive inhabitants of the most ancient city on Hissarlik, together with very numerous stone implements and stone weapons, the following metals: gold, silver, lead, copper, but no iron; in fact, no trace of this latter metal was ever found by me either in any of the pre-

historic cities of Troy, or at Mycenae. Nothing, I think, could better

testify to the great antiquity of the pre-historic ruins at Hissarlik and at

Mycenae, than the total absence of iron."

While digging at Ilion, Schliemann felt that the level of culture

had deteriorated as time went on, he felt this way he said because the

lower strata contained artifacts of finer quality. Furthermore, these

people were all "Aryan" in race, because designs such as the swastika

inscribed on various small objects, particularly on whorls, reminded

him and other he consulted of religious motifs found in India.

Schliemann was wise enough to consult an expert about the

techniques of manufacturing shown by his unique collection of delicate

jewelry. Carlo Giuliano, a famous London goldsmith and connoisseur

of antiques, found that the gold was in general very pure (up to 23

carats fine) and that the craftsmen had been expert in making thin wire,

punching complicated patterns from gold leaf and soldering

microscopic beads (granulation). But "how the primitive goldsmith

could do all this fine work... without the aid of a lens... is an enigma

even to Mr. Giuliano." But it wasn't performed without the aid of a lens

because we have by now found many convex and concave lens from

antiquity."   -Progress Into the Past, William A. McDonald

A bronze bull was discovered at a hilltop shrine near Til fit in

the hill country, cited as Proto-Israelite in origin. One fresco from the

ruins of Mari, a city of the Semetic-speaking Amorites situated on the

Syria-Iraq border and standing on the west bank of the Euphrates river,

shows Baal as a bull 'striding on top of mountains', expressing the

powerful connection between the bull of heaven and mountains.

The Achaeans ranked Zeus and Poseidon as immortals;

picturing both as armed with the thunderbolt, once wielded by Rhea, and in the Minoan and Mycenaean religions withheld from male use. Poseidon's trident and Zeus's thunderbolt were originally the same weapon, the sacred labrys, or double-axe, but became distinguished from each other when Zeus claimed sole right to the thunderbolt. Poseidon's thunderbolt was converted into a three-pronged fish-spear, his chief devotees having turned seafarers; whereas Zeus retained his as a symbol of supreme sovereignty. Poseidon's name was sometimes spelled Potidan, which may shed light on the origin of his name. It may have been borrowed from that of his goddess-mother, after whom the city of Potidaea was called: 'the water-goddess of Ida' - Ida meaning any wooded mountain.

The Mycenaean word ponike means red and has the suffix of the name of a Greek goddess, Nike. Nike is known as the messenger between men and god and is shaped in the form of a mushroom with wings outstretched as if her feathers were gills. Ponike is a Mycenaean word relating to the colour of a mushroom. The Phoenicians are said to have derived their name from the word ponike.

In the Bible two Hebrew words are used to denote man; the first is "adom;" the second is "eesh." Since both are translated as "man" in the English texts laymen cannot distinguish between them. But note how they are used differently in Genesis. When Genesis quotes God as saying that he would create man in his image it does not use the word eesh; it use adom. "Let us make adom in our image..." It does not say, "Let us make eesh in our image..." "God formed adom out of the dust of the Earth," not eesh. Adom became a living soul, not eesh. "In the days that God man adom, in the likeness of God he made them..." Not him, but them, in the likeness of God, he made the Red Ones.

Adom being a living soul is obviously alluding to the mushroom being alive, out of the dust obviously alluding to the ground, and when you ingest it you see god obviously alluding to the awesome power and intensity of the mind expanding experience provided by this carefully prepared mushroom. There are other passages that distinguish between man being adom as a specially created being in the image of God, and man or woman as eesh or eesha as a creature of the Earth. This strongly correlates with the Egyptian ankh that was in the shape of a man.

Further insight into the red color associated with Adam is provided by the Phoenicians, those cousins of the Hebrews who lived along the shores of the Meditteranean just north of the Holy Land in the cities of Tyre and Sidon. The Phoenicians had extremely close ties with the Hebrews, trading extensively with them, providing lumber for the building of Solomon's temple, and Phoenician language was essentially Hebrew, no more different in dialect than is found today among various regional groups in the United States.

Phoinikes for the people and Phoinike for the region are terms used which have references found as far back as Homeric times. There is an obvious link between these terms and the common noun phoinix, to the feminine adjective po-ni-ki-ja (2nd millennium B.C. Mycenaean texts), meaning "red" and referring to a chariot.

This really caught my attention when I remembered that other cultures around the ancient world had mythologies concerning flying vessels or chariots, in the East they have flying 'Vimanas,' today people are using the 'Vimanas' as supposed textual evidence of ancient flying saucers, I believe by persons who know that Vimanas or 'flaming red chariots' were simply the Amanita muscaria mushroom. Carl Jung mentions Indian flying chariots in regards to Alchemy, not aliens. Every ignorant facet of Ufology is linked to religion.

Cuneiform texts of the 2nd millennium show, the word "Canaan" is also linked with the concept of "red." The snake was repulsive to Hebrews. Archeology reveals that snakes played a bizarre role in the worship ceremony of the Canaanites, Israel's ancient enemy. Thus the snake made an ideal evil symbol for the biblical writer.

"A series of Italian archaelological missions promoted by the University of Rome and then by the Italian National Research Council have revealed a good deal about the Phoenicians on the island of Pantelleria (Kossyra) and on Malta, where the discovery of the sanctuary at Tas Silg has yielded conclusive proof that several civizations followed one another on the same site: prehistoric, Phoenician, Greek, and Roman." The most significant Italian discoveries are without a doubt those made in Sicily and Sardinia. In Sicily, excavations at Motya by the two institutions mentioned above and the local Monuments and Fine Arts Service have brought to light a tophet with over a thousand stelae bearing figures that provide a great deal of information about Phoenician art. Large numbers of inscribed stelae bearing figures have been recovered at Carthage and other North African centers (Sousse [Susah] and Constantine) from a special type of sanctuary, called tophet, in which children were sacrificed. In the area of today's Tunisia, an early tophet was discovered; and another when we enter Algeria.

In Sardinia, the 1962 discovery of Monte Sirai, a fortress built inland from the coastal town of Sulcis, provides evidence of military penetration on the island. In turn, the excavations at Antas show the encounter between a Roman cult and an earlier Phoenician cult (that of the god Sid) attested to by over twenty inscriptions. More current finds are those being made at Tharros, the large Phoenician center near present-day Oristano, at the point where the ships coming in from Africa met the route for the Balearic Islands and Spain. Here, walls erected to provide a powerful defensive system have been discovered, along with a tophet and stelae of unusual size and form. A fundamental change occured in Phoenicia with the 3rd millennium B.C. The "urban revolution" reached this coastal area, where for the first time a group of sanctuaries, dwellings and public buildings that could be called a city came into being. The scene of this new experience was again Byblos. Favored by a geographical position that made it the natural trading station along the routes between the Syro-Palestinian coast and Egypt, Byblos was able to absorb and assimilate the innovatory elements coming from Mesopotamia (The Euphrates River), northern Syria and the Nile valley.

Byblos became a highly developed urban settlement. Served by two ports, the city was protected inland by a massive defensive wall which enclosed an extensive residential area. Two large sanctuaries, known as the "L-shaped Building" and the "Temple of the Lady of Byblos," were its principal places of worship. They yielded the most important artistic documents of this period, such as the characteristic zoomorphic pottery with geometric decorations.

From the time of the 2nd Egyptian dynasty, at the beginning of the 3rd millennium, traders from the Delta area came to Byblos for

supplies of timber, metals and valuable goods and around 2600 B.C.
there was even an Egyptian temple in the city. The importance of
Byblos for Egypt is confirmed by the fact that the city appears in the
myth of Isis who comes there looking for the body of Osiris, cast into
the sea by Set.

   At the end of the 3rd millennium relations between Byblos and
Egypt came to an abrupt hault, so that an Egyptian text of the time,
known as The Lamentations of Ipu-wer, was forced to note: "Today no
one sails north to Byblos any more. How will we get cedar for our
mummies?" It is no coincidence that Assyrian and Egyptian
inscriptions mention the desire to procure timber from Byblos. In the
9th century B.C., for instance, Ashurnasirpal II says in an inscription at
Balawat: "I marched as far as Mount Lebanon, and felled cedar,
cypress and juniper trees. With the cedar trunks, I made the roof of this
temple; with cedar wood I made the leaves of the doors and covered
them with sheets of bronze, attaching them to the doors."

- The Phoenicians (1988)

   From what I learned about these very important and intriguing
peoples is this. Their whole routine was acting exactly as the most
cunning merchants; they would obtain precious metals like silver
(especially large amounts from Iberia) and gold; others as well i.e.,
copper, tin and bronze. But the great part about it was this; they would
trade further inland with the inhabitants of the region who didn't know
how to work with the metals. So it should be obvious now that the
Phoenicians expansion down around the coast of the Mediterranean was
due mainly to their ability of trading relatively cheap food items for
precious metals in large quantities and then trading that gold and other

items to civilizations like Egypt that would pay much more for the precious metals than those who the Phoenicians acquired it from.

Diodorus Siculus says "the far West, with its wealth of metals, was the original objective of Phoenician expansion." And as to the Iberian Peninsula as an essential reason for trade, "The country has the most numerous and excellent silver mines... The natives do not know how to use the metal. But the Phoenicians, experts in commerce, would buy this silver in exchange for some other small goods. Consequently taking the silver to Greece, Asia, and all other peoples, the Phoenicians made great earnings. Thus practicing this trade for a long time, they became rich, and founded many colonies, some in Sicily and on the neighboring islands, others in Libya, Sardinia and Iberia."

"Testimonies from the Old Testament were much fuller, especially when it came to relations with Tyre, and to Solomon's times, when the Tyrian king, Hiram I, had the temple of Solomon built in Jerusalem. Later, relations between the kings of Israel and the kings of Tyre extended to religious matters, such as the influence on Israel exerted by Phoenician polytheism. The word "Sidonians" is used in both the Old Testament and in Homeric poems as a synonym for "Phoenicians."

Reflecting the political and cultural influence of Egypt over Phoenicia, in the pantheon of Byblos we find other identifications with Egyptian deities. El, portrayed on Hellenistic coins with two pairs of wings, according to an iconography also familiar to Philo, was considered identical to Ra, the pharoah's god; Reshef is probably to be identified with the god who in certain texts of the Old Kingdom is given the name Khai-Tau ("He who appears surrounded by flames"), while

Baal Shamaim is probably called Seth, the name which the Egyptian account of Wenamon attributes to the main god of Byblos.

Our documentation then leads us to the 2nd century A.D., when the treatise De Syria Dea, attributed to Lucian, describes an enormous celebration held in Byblos in honour of Adonis, whose story takes place in the city. The name of the character is obviously Semitic (adon or adonai), and is frequently used to refer to male deities with the generic meaning of "lord"; it never appears in Phoenician inscriptions used as a proper name.

Greek and Latin sources tell the story of a young hunter of great beauty, born of incest; the beautiful Adonis is loved and fought over by two goddesses, Aphrodite and Persephone. In classical mythology Adonis dies while hunting, killed by a wild boar and Aphrodite and her followers create the mourning ritual that characterized the celebration of the Adoniad festival.

In the Greek and Roman world this was celebrated by the women in a private way, on the rooftops, with lamentations, sexual license and the creation of small "gardens" made up of short-lived plants. In Byblos the celebration took place in the sanctuary of Aphrodite, with public mourning ceremonies, tonsure of women or ritual prostitution, the liturgy or the "awakening" of Adonis, who was considered alive even after his experience of death. In Byblos, therefore, the worship of Adonis was very different from the ritual veneration of the god in Greece from the 7th century B.C. onwards. We have further evidence of this in a lengthy Greek inscription from the 4th century B.C. It is a decree allowing Cypriots resident in Athens to celebrate their own Adoniads "according to the customs of their homeland": the ritual was part of the worship of Aphrodite of Cyprus and was celebrated in forms that are directly reminiscent of what we know about the Adoniads of Phoenicia.

Going from Byblos to our documentation on Tyre, the first observation concerns the extreme poverty of direct epigraphic documentation. The best document we have is the list of deities invoked as guarantors of the treaty signed in 675 B.C. between Baal, king of Tyre, and Esarhaddon, king of Assyria. There are also two new names: Eshmun and Melqarth. In Tyre, Melqarth was the main city deity, for his name means "King of the City"; in a bilingual Maltese inscription his name is accompanied by the definition "Baal of Tyre" and by the Greek epithet archegetes. Melqarth appears for the first time in an Aramaic inscription of the 9th century B.C., in which Bar Hadad, king of Damascus, dedicates a votive tablet to him. But the cult of Melqarth in Tyre dates back at least to the 10th century when, according to Josephus, who quotes Menander of Ephesus, King Hiram had a sanctuary built in his honour, and another in honour of Astarte, on the ruins of some earlier temples; Hiram was also the first to celebrate festivities in honour of Melqarth.

Dedications to Melqarth appear also in Cyprus, Carthage, Sicily, Sardinia, Malta, and Spain and his sanctuaries accompanied the overall Phoenician expansion and marked the navigation routes. Melqarth was very early on identified with the Greek Heracles and much of the information we have on this god and his worship has come down to us with that name. He was the son of Zeus (perhaps a Baal of the heavens) and of Asteria (Astarte in an astral translation). Like Adonis and Melqarth, Eshmun is not documented before the 1st *millennium B.C., and it seems likely that his origin is similar to theirs, as an evolution of earlier Syrian tradition. This god's name, in fact, seems to derive etymologically from the Semetic word for "oil," which in both Ebla and Ugarit we find used as a divine name in the cult. This hypothesis is supported by archaeological findings and by the classical interpretations, all of which identiy Eshmun with Asclepius, the god of medicine. Just like Adonis and Melqarth, Eshmun is portrayed in our classical sources as a god who dies and then returns to life.*

While we know of no Pheonician word to indicate what we call "religion," the term qodesh was probably the equivalent of our concept of "sacred," in the widest semantic sense. This term meant both "to consecrate" and "consecrated," "holy" and "sanctuary," and referred to persons involved in the worship, offerings, sacred places, and deities. The generic term for a deity is el (or il), which becomes elat in the feminine gender. But this was also the proper name of a god, whom we know primarily from the myths of Ugarit as the Supreme Being. Baal is used quite normally as a generic term meaning "lord" or "master" and applied to various male deities. Similarly, on Mount Tabor, also in Roman times, there was a widespread worship of a mountain Baal identified with Zeus. We also find evidence of the worship of these local Baals in the writings of Philo, who confirms the important position held constantly by another Baal, seen as the dominator of the sky and the master of lightning.

This is Baal Shamaim, the "Lord of the Heavens," considered one of the main gods of Byblos as earl as the 10th century B.C. We find him again at Tyre, Cyprus, Carthage and in Sardinia, always in a very exalted hierarchical position.

In Byblos, a much older temple probably dated from the first
quarter of the 2nd millenium B.C.- the period when Byblos was ruled
by an Amorite dynasty, was consecrated to the worship of a goddess
called Baalath, "mistress" and "sovereign" of the city of Byblos,
mentioned in Akkadian and Egyptian documents of the 2nd millennium
B.C. and still famous in the 2nd millenium A.D. with the name
Aphrodite. A series of royal inscriptions are evidence of her supremacy
and her role as the protectress of the reigning dynasty. The Baalath of
Byblos was portrayed with all the symbolic attributes of the Egyptian
Hathor-Isis, with whom for centuries she was identified; in King
Yehawmilk's votive stele she has horns on her head and bears the disc
and a crowned uraeus (headdress in the form of the sacred serpent),
while Egyptian texts from the Middle Kingdom equate Hathor, "Lady of
Byblos," with the Egyptian "Lady of Dendera."

-The Phoenicians (1988)

Chapter Four: Sun-Worship & Biblical Historical Character Association with Egyptian Figures

"The implausible yarn about the birth and life of Moses, as has been hitherto presented in the Old Testament, has perpetually confounded and vexed the minds of researchers. His Egyptian name, his privileged upbringing in the royal house of pharaoh, his status, his "serpent staff" in the desert, his expulsion, his meeting with the god of Israel that he does not recognize, his monomania for freeing the "chosen people" (when they had never been captives), have never been satisfactorily explained - until now. Moses' brother was Aaron and he has been linked to the pharaoh Smenkhare, considered by some to have been the brother of Akhenaton."   -Anonymous

"...the so-called Five Books of Moses are the literary product of an age much later than the one in which Moses is supposed to have lived... little research reveals that there was nothing new with the story of this "Moses." A little digging into the mythology of the Persians, Babylonians, Chaldeans, Indians, and Assyrians, and we discover the entire tale presented on the life of this "Moses" to be a plagiarization of much earlier myths of solar heroes such as the Babylonian Nebo and Babylonian Lord Sargon who had lived over 2,000 years before Moses. We can conclude that the story of Moses was concocted in somewhat of a hurry and without much care. Utility was what mattered and the fact that the cover story was workable. The Jewish myth mongers simply adopted the anecdotes and transposed them onto their own concocted fictive character, a mythographic personality who had no physical existence. Their Moses was a stand-in for someone else, for a true-life

figure that was not to be exposed to the light... The Assyrian prince Sargon also, being pursued by his uncle, is said to have been abandoned on the Euphrates in a basket made of reeds, to have been found by a water-carrier, and to have been brought up by him" - a story the Jews have interwoven into the account of the life of their fabulous Moses" – Arthur Dewes (The Christ Myth)

"They tell you that Moses never lived. I acquiesce. If they tell me that the story that came from Egypt is mythology, I shall not protest; it is mythology. They tell me that the book of Isaiah, as we have it today, is composed of writings of at least three and perhaps four different periods: I knew it before they ever told me, before they knew it"

- Rabbi Emil Hirsch

"The figure of Osarsiph-Moses is clearly modelled on the historic memory of Akhenaten."

Donald Redford is no lightweight. He is professor of Egyptology at the University of Toronto, and is the author of several books and key articles on the Amarna period and ancient Egypt's association with Western Asia. His findings must be taken seriously. This intrigues me because Sigmund Freud's last book was titled "Moses and Monotheism" where he explains his belief in the connection between Moses and Akhenaten.

The novel worship of the Sun as All-father seems to have been brought to the Northern Aegean by the fugitive priesthood of the monotheistic Akhenaton, in the fourteenth century B.C., and grafted upon the local cults; hence Orpheus' s alleged visit to Egypt. Later Orphic priests, who wore Egyptian costume, called the demi-god whose raw bull' s flesh they ate "Dionysus", and reserved the name Apollo for the immortal Sun.

Akhenaten was known as a heretic because he switched Egypt away from the pantheon of gods it previously worshipped and therefore switched power away from the priest that held sway over the entire empire. The price Akhenaten paid for abandoning the old gods was terrible. Under the orders of the military general Horebheb, who took the throne after Aye's brief four-year reign, the city of Akhetaten was dismantled right down to its foundations. All reference to the dreaded Aten was expunged from inscriptions, and statues of Akhenaten were buried or destroyed. Moreover, Horemheb had the names of the four Amarna kings – Akhenaten, Smenkhkare, Tutankhamun, and Aye – struck from official records, and extended back his own reign to begin in the year that Akhenaten's father, Amenhotep III, initiated a co-regency with his son. Therefore Akhenaten's memory, and indeed that of his successors, was banished entirely from Egypt; he was never to be mentioned again by name. In legal documents dating from Horemheb's reign there is reference only to the time of 'the rebel' or the 'criminal of Akhetaten'.

The most powerful religion in Egypt before this period was that of the Theban god Amun, or Amun-re, whose main temple was in Karnak, located a few kilometres north of Thebes (modern Luxor). Its priesthood presided over all rites of kingship in Upper Egypt and held immense sway over the royal family. To see their power, influence and revenues stripped away virtually overnight could not have pleased them, and it would have been a similar story at temples all over the empire. Akhenaten's reign ended suddenly, no one knows why, his dream lasted for just twelve to thirteen years. After the brief reign of his successor Smenkhkare, the restoration of the old religions began in earnest under the next king's (Tut-ankh-aten) advisors, around this time he changed his name to Tut.ankh.amun as well as his wife Ankhesenpaaten to Ankhesenamun.

You might recall the Ankhesenamun character from the Hollywood film, 'The Mummy.'

"Strangely enough, Smenkhkare is not mentioned in any textual inscriptions, nor is he depicted in any form, until he is elevated suddenly to the position of King of Upper and Lower Egypt towards the end of Ahkenaten's reign. It is most likely that he is a son of Amenhotep III, although his mother remains a mystery. It is conceivable also that Tutankhamun, who was himself never depicted in art before his ascension to the throne, was likewise a brother or half-brother to both Akhenaten and Smenkhkare...Tutankhaten cannot have been any more than nine years old at this time, and so the day-to-day running of the country was placed in the hands of others more capable. General Horemheb became the king's Deputy and Regent, taking charge of military and political affairs from Memphis, while Aye, Akhenaten's oldest vizier, became the boy-king's personal adviser and the administrator of all matters relating to religion. Tutankhaten married the king's second eldest surviving daughter, Ankh.es.en.pa.aten, whom Akh.en.aten had already taken as his chief royal wife following Merit.aten's marriage to Smenkh.ka.re...The only textual evidence that sheds light on Tutankh(aten/amun)'s parentage is a granite lion statue found at Soleb in northern Sudan, ancient Nubia. It bears an inscription in which the boy-king makes reference to his 'father Nebmaatre Amenhotep', i.e. Amenhotep III, who is known to have constructed twin

temples at Soleb, one for himself and the other for the Great Royal Wife, Tiye. They were both completed by Tutankhamun as an expression of his descent from Amenhotep III, as opposed to the heretic Akhenaten. Yet even though Tutankhamun and his wife Ankhesenamun would appear to have abandoned the Aten faith focused on the city of Akhetaten, it was quite clear from several key objects found in his tomb that both he and his wife continued to venerate the Aten throughout their lifetimes. In fact, the young pharaoh did little, if anything, to quell the Amarna heresy...Located in the depths of Sudan, the ancient kingdom of Nubia, the father of Akhenaten (Amenhotep IV) and Tutankhamun, Amenhotep III, constructed twin temples at Soleb. One temple was for himself and the other his Great Royal Wife, Tiye. In his own temple dedicated to the God Amun, are a series of columns on which are inscribed various African and Asiatic place names. One of which reads t3 ssw yhw, 'Yahweh in the land of the Shasu'. Referred to in Egyptian textual accounts as 'the land of Shasu', Edom is the highlands region that stretched between the Gulf of Aqaba in the south and the Dead Sea in the north. The above reference to Yahweh is the oldest on record. Egyptian textual inscriptions also link the Shasu specifically with Mount Seir, the chief peak in the Seir range, and with Edom. Originally, the Bible tells us Seir was the homeland of the Emim, said to be descended from the Nephilim."

- Tutankhamun Exodus Conspiracy

"From predynastic times the pharaohs of Egypt were in the habit of considering themselves personifications of the sun. The strange idea had been vogue for thousands of years. It was, therefore, not a massive change when Akhenaton, the so-called first "monotheist,"

decided that he too was a personification of the solar orb. It was not this theory that was so obnoxious to the Egyptian priests and people, but the contemptuous and irreverent manner in which he enforced his dogma that caused them so much consternation and that ultimately compelled them to rid themselves of this most "meddlesome" priest.

So when we hear it admitted that Christianity owes a great deal to Akhenaton's monotheistic cult we need to reflect and understand that it does not stop there. Christianity is based not only on Akhenaton's particular skewed version of solar theology, but on Egyptian sun worship of every sort. Splitting hairs over the matter and indicting one particular late version of the form of veneration does not change this fact, it merely emphasizes it. Author Ralph Ellis (following on from the great Comyns Beaumont) has a slightly different opinion regarding Akhenaton and Smenkhare. He suggests that Akhenaton was Aaron and that Tuthmosis (a mysterious first brother to Akhenaton that official historians have been curiously vague and dismissive about) was Moses. We can presume it more likely, after perusing the revisionist scholars, that Akhenaton himself makes a more logical prototype for the man Jesus than his son/half brother Tutankhamen. After all, one of the titles of Akhenaton was "Son of the Sun" (or "Son of God"). His wife Nefertiti would then make a good approximation of Mary Magdalene. It is an intriguing theory to mull over. Each reader and researcher must come to their own conclusions over the various biographical discrepancies."   - Dan Russell

"An Italian artist of the late fifteenth century seems to have been aware of the secret meaning of the fiery winged serpent in his depiction of the same event. The painting shows a fiery serpent

attacking the Israelites. The serpent is directly under a tree, where one finds the fly agaric. Its back, or top, is red with white spots and a convex curve in the manner of a mushroom; his underside is not only white like the mushroom's underside is but also has thin, protruding scales that resemble mushroom gills. The beast looks directly at the viewer with a conspiratorial smile on his face. The two lower victims, already dealt with by the monster, have the look of wishing they were dead; the one with his fingers on his chest looks as though he is about to vomit.

Weigall's 'Tutankhamen And Other Essays' carried a reasonable account of the life and times of Tutankhamun, yet he went further. After describing Akhenaten's rise to power, he began extolling the virtues of the intangible, formless Aten, seeing it in terms of an archaic representation of 'the worship of the true God, almost as we understand him now'. He drew attention to the uncanny similarities between Psalm 104 and the so-called 'Hymn to the Aten', an ode to the omnipotent powers of the sun-disk, often said to have been composed by Akhenaten himself. For Weigall it was 'undoubted the original of our 104th Psalm, many of the verses of which are in the hieroglyphic script are almost word for word those of the Hebrew version'.

The covenants between god and Moses were in fact covenants between Aton and Akhenaton. This revelation gives incredible relevance to the passages from the early books of the Bible. To understand the world of the past and the world of today it is essential that the passages are, for the most part, seen to be references to Earthly and political intrigues and not spiritual ones.

The exposure of the fraud concerning the lineage of Isaac

places us on guard concerning every other aspect of the Abraham story. If anyone was "fathering" nations it appears to have been the pharaohs. Abraham was father of three different divisions of people; through Hagar the bond-maiden he became the father of the Ishmaelites, the Arabs, millions of them. Through another bond-maiden, Keturah, he became the father of other countless millions of eastern Hebrews, many of them living today in India; and only through Sarah, his rightful wife, did he become the father of the "Children of the Promise."

- Fredrick Haberman

(Tracing Our Ancestors)

"The great Yuya was not only the appointed vizier to the pharaoh Tuthmosis IV, his dream-analyst and keeper of his granaries, etc, etc, but he was also the son-in-law of the high priest of the Solar Cult. Revisionist historians have also revealed that Aye, the uncle of Akhenaton and pharaoh after Tutankhamun was the son of Joseph the patriarch of the Levites (Jews).

"They have proven that Joseph's daughter Tiye was married to pharaoh Amenhotep III, the father of Akhenaton; that Tuthmosis III was the prototype for King David, and that Amenhotep III was the prototype for King Solomon.

Noel Streatfeild continues: *'The more you read the more you realize that almost nothing is known about Tutankhamen. What I have attempted is to bring him alive for children up to twelve years from what sketchy knowledge there is."*

On the back of her book, 'The Boy Pharoah', it says: 'Noel Streatfeild was born in Sussex. Her father was Bishop of Lewes. She is a great-great-granddaughter of Elizabeth Fry. For four hundred years the family lived in the village of Chiddingstone in Kent, now National Trust property. She went to a prestigious acting school and then traveled extensively while doing stage work.

In 1929 her father died, so she gave up the uncertain stage life and wrote her first novel, which was called THE WHICHARTS. She wrote her first book for children in 1935 and called it BALLET SHOES.'

If any woman was privy to a great deal of knowledge concerning hidden academics in religion, it would be this woman. Let me share with you some of the things I read in her book. Regarding the origin of the Earth she states: 'The most universally respected of the ancient Egyptian gods was called Osiris. He had a human head. Most primitive people have made up stories to explain how the world began.

The Egyptians' story was that to begin there was no Earth, only sea. On the sea floated an egg. From it the god of the sun was born. This god of the sun became father to four children who between them ruled the world. They were called Osiris, Isis, Seth and Nepthys.

In course of time Osiris inherited his father's throne from which he governed the world with great goodness and distinction, so he was much loved. The love of the people for Osiris made his brother Seth so deadly jealous that one day he murdered him, then cut him into small pieces which he buried all over Egypt. Osiris's wife Isis, helped by a god called Anubis, collected all the pieces of Osiris together.

"...The immediate predecessor of Tutankhamen, called Amenhotep IV, worshipped Aton (Sun) to the exclusion of all other gods. In fact he so believed in Aton that he tried to force his belief on the whole country. But, as we know, the ancient Egyptians were

conservative and stubborn and not willing to give up their old gods, so during Tutankhamen's reign the absolute worship of Aton passed and the old gods came back into favour.' Favour which never really left them."

Mary (the Mother of Jesus) may be based upon Nefertiti or Akhenaton's second wife Kiyah who was also known as Mery, meaning "beloved."(A friend once told me that Kiya is vernacular in Rastafarian for Cannabis. (Author)) Mary Magdalene has been traced back to Ankhsenpaaten, the wife of Smenkhare.

"In the case of the patriarch Saul (suggestively a name also used for Paul, the founder of Christianity) we have the truth laid before us with such clarity that it amazes us that the cover on the box of the Judeo-Christian jig-saw has not been witnessed before now. Saul is quite clearly a rendering of Sol, the name for the sun. The mythographers added his spurious life-story as an accent to suggest, as subtly as they were able, that King David's line was a continuation of the Sol Cult. Furthermore, it has been finally proven that the Aton-worshipping "monotheist" Akhenaton was the prototype for the biblical Moses."

-Michael Tsarion excerpts from

"The Irish Origins of Civilization"

In the old texts that are contemporaneous with the Latin translation of the Turba there are gruesome recipes in the manner of the Magic Papyri, as for instance the drying of a man over a heated stone, the cutting off of hands and feet, etc. Remember than the Egyptians made the hieroglyph of the mushroom in the image of a man, this correlates directly with many texts that indicate the drying of the

Amanita muscaria is done over a slow fire, or a heated stone. The
cutting off of hands and feet remind me of the slaying of the dragon and
the cutting off of the lion's paws. The moral of the story is obviously
this, that you must neutralize the deadly attributes of the Amanita,
meaning the ibotenic acid, before consumption.

Orpheus is said by Diodorus Siculus to have used the old
thirteen-consonant alphabet; and the legend that he made the trees move
and charmed wild beasts apparently refers to its sequence of seasonal
trees and symbolic animals. As sacred king he was struck by a
thunderbolt – that is, killed with a double-axe – in an oak grove at the
summer solstice, and then dismembered by the Maenads of the bull
cult, like Zagreus. This Orpheus did not come in conflict with the cult
of Dionysus; he was Dionysus, thus Proclus writes: Orpheus, because
he was the principal in the Dionysian rites, is said to have suffered the
same fate as the god. And Apollodorus credits him with having invented
the Mysteries of Dionysus.

Herodotus mentions that the Egyptians, who inhabit the
marshes of the Nile, gather water-lilies that they call the lotus. These
grow in great abundance when the river is full, flooding the neighboring
flats, and after they are gathered they are then left to dry in the sun.
Afterward, from the center of each blossom they pick out something
which resembles a poppy-head, grind it, and make it into loaves which
they bake. The root of this plant is also edible; it is round, about as big
as an apple, and tastes fairly sweet. There is another kind of lily to be
found in the river; this resembles a rose, and its fruit is formed on a
separate stalk from that which bears the blossom, and has very much
the look of a wasps' comb. The fruit contains a number of seeds, about

the size of an olive stone, which are good to eat either fresh or dried. (This lotus is psychoactive.)

"The ancient world's greatest collector of magical books was Ptolemy III of Egypt (246-221 BC). He had the profound insight to order all travelers who disembarked at Alexandria to deposit any books in their possession at the Royal Library for copying, the traveller then receiving the copy, the Library keeping the original. This rule applied even to official state copies of classical tragedies from Athens, the Library preferring to forfeit the large pledge rather than part with the original. The Royal Library, thus, over the course of hundreds of years, became the greatest library in the world, possessed of hundreds of thousands of priceless volumes, easily the greatest cultural treasure of the ancient world.

The Ptolemies made this vast treasure available to the scholars studying at or visiting the Museum. These included Erasistratos (medicine), Theocritus (poety), Euclid (geometry), Archimedes (mathematical physics), Ctesibius (mechanics), Eratosthenes (Mathematical geography), Callimachus (poetry), Apollonius (mathematical astronomy), Apollonius Rhodius (poetry), Herophilus (anatomy and pharmacology), Hero (mechanical physics), Aristarchus (astronomy), Hipparchus (astronomy) and Strato (physics, natural science).

Erasistratos discovered the valves of the Heart, the nervous system, peristalsis and the capillary system. Eratosthenes calculated the circumference of the Earth to within an error of less than one percent. Hero invented the steam engine and the mechanical windmill. Hipparchus invented trigonometry. Ctesibius invented the force pump and the constant-head water clock. Aristarchus of Samos propounded an accurate picture of the heliocentric universe nineteen centuries before Copernicus. Euclid, of course, and Archimedes virtually invented geometry and physics, or, at least, are the effective vehicles for the transmission of the technical tradition they inherited at Alexandria and Syracuse.

Zenobia, in a bid for Christian and Egyptian support in her fight with Aurelian, incinerated most of the work of these seminal geniuses when she sacked the Royal Library. Alexandria's Christian authorities destroyed most of what remained. Nothing at all survives from Ctesibius, Aristarchus, Herophilus, Erasistratos, Strato and many of the legendary predecessors of Euclid and Archimedes, and only fragments survive from most of the others. We know of them from surviving writers like Aristotle, Theophrastus, Galen and Ptolemy.

It took human culture more than a millennium to recover the science burned at the Museum, and most of the poetry, drama and mythology, the spectacular genius of Classical Greece, including most of Aristotle's huge library, is lost forever. Imagine having the books used by Aristotle. We have about a tenth of the plays of Aischylos, Sophokles and Euripides, and they're nearly all masterpieces." Thoth Hermes Trismegistus, the founder of Egyptian learning, the Wise Man of the ancient world, gave to the priests and philosophers of antiquity the secrets which have been preserved to this day in myth and legend. These allegories and emblematic figures conceal the secret formula for spiritual, mental, moral, and physical regeneration commonly known as the Mystic Chemistry of the Soul (alchemy).

The mysteries of Hermeticism, the great spiritual truths hidden

from the world by the ignorance of the world, and the keys of the secret
doctrines of the ancient philosophers, are all symbolized by the Virgin
Isis. The ancients gave the name Isis to one of their occult medicines;
the original alchemist were without a doubt followers of Isis. Her black
drape also signifies that the moon, or the lunar humidity--the sophic
universal mercury and the operating substance of Nature in alchemical
terminology--has no light of its own, but receives its light, its fire, and
its vitalizing force from the sun. Isis was the image or representative of
the Great Works of the wise men: the Philosopher's Stone, the Elixir of
Life, and the Universal Medicine.

The authorities surrounded the Tree of Life with fearsome
Cherubim and flaming swords, so that all would be afraid to taste the
fruit of gnosis, now subject to prohibitio, as so clearly explained by this
brilliant shaman, floating, as they said, on "the cold, flowing waters of
the Lake of Mnemosyne." One 13th century Gnostic-Christian fresco,
pg 107, from Plaincouralt Chapel, pictures Eve, her hands cupped over
her womb, with a snake's tail, standing next to a giant Amanita
muscaria, speckled cap and all, around which curls the sacred snake.
In the Gnostic-Christian frescoes discovered in 1919 in the Tomb of the
Aurelii in Rome, dating to c.230 CE, the snake, curled around the Tree
of Life, is portrayed the same way, with its mouth open, in the attitude
of the instructor."

"The word 'Messiah,' 'Saviour,' 'Anointed one,' is the traditional
title given to King David, a war shaman, and to all kings of his line. To
claim to be the Moshiy'a, in Greek Khristos, was in no way
blasphemous in Hebrew eyes. The Greek Khrestos, meaning 'good,' was
an appellation of the mystery gods, and is obviously cognate with

Khristos, 'anointed one.' The anointed ceremony was performed for both the King and the High Priest, who had the title, even in Roman times, of 'Priest Messiah.'

In 415 Archbishop Cyril of Alexandria arranged the savage murder of Hypatia by a mob led by his Nitrian monks. She was the daughter of Theon, a legendary philosopher and mathematician who "interpreted astronomical works, and the writings of Hermes Trismegistus and Orpheus." Hypatia was reputed, by her student Synesius of Cyrene, Bishop of Ptolemais, to be the greatest astronomer and mathematician alive. Her murder had precisley the effect Cyril intended; the best of the remaining scholars at the Museum left Alexandria, never to return. We know Hypatia only by legend because 'the city of orthodox' cordinated the destruction of all her writings, along with numerous other legendary, and popular, Hermetic and alchemical tracts.

The fruit, the sacrament, the pharmakon, was the major point of Gnostic disagreement with the Orthodox church, since the Gnostic apotheosis consisted not of the ordinary symbolic communion, but of a second pharmacological sacrament of apolytrosis (deliverance, liberation, redemption). The pharmacological serpent, with vine and golden fleece, ushers Iaion (Ia-ion) into the presence of 'the Mother.' Athena holds the prophetic owl she inherited from Lilith the Transformer. She also wears the Gorgoneion, symbol of the terrifying mysteries through which the naked soul must pass before it is admitted "into the Father, into the Mother, Jesus of the infinite sweetness."

Aldous Huxley used the ancient Sanskrit equivalent of apolytrosis, moksha, to describe the central sacrament - entheogenic mushroom juice – of his utopian Island. That, of course, is a historically accurate reference to the Rg Veda.

This split of original Christianity into two rival churches (the semi-suppressed mystical versions and the dominant church of the false gospel) fits perfectly with the burgeoning new view, which I maintain, that there are two rival mysticisms: false mysticism/spirituality, which reveres religious experiencing without the crutch of drugs, and true mysticism/spirituality, true religion, which reveres entheogens wholeheartedly and emphatically as the premiere door to heaven, to religious and high philosophical fulfillment. Entheogenic fundamentalism is the belief that those who refuse to eat and drink the sacred plant, which is the flesh of God, condemn themselves to eternal torment, eternal unquenched thirst and unfulfillment, and separation from God.

The Church organized the Imperial murder of many leading Gnostics and the systematic destruction of nearly all their writings. The lost Gnostic writings were known only by their titles and distorted legend for the better part of two milennia, but by a spectacular archeological miracle fifty-two Gnostic texts, thirty of them complete and unknown except by legend, were rediscovered on leather-bound papyrus scrolls in 1945 at Nag Hammadi in central Egypt. They were written in Coptic, phonetic Egyptian, Greek transliterations of the original Greek.

The scrolls had been buried in jars, about 370 CE, in meditation caves, obviously in fear of their discovery. Since there was no war going on at the time, it is assumed that the regular authorities were involved. In his Easter letter of 367, the supreme regular authority, Archbishop Athanasius of Alexandria, condemned heretics and their "apocryphal books to which they attribute antiquity and give the name of saints." That, of course, is a perfect description of the Nag Hammadi texts, many of which are copies of works hundreds of years older.

In Hebrew se'ir means 'rough coating', Seir was also the land of Esau, 'the father of the Edomites in Mount Seir'. Azazel is a fallen angel, whose name came to be associated with the word 'scapegoat' in Bible translations. While looking for a word in The American Heritage College Dictionary Third Edition, I saw a picture of a mushroom and immediately flipped back to the page it was on and read the words 'destroying angel'. Its definition is: Any of several poisonous mushrooms of the genus Amanita. Azazel in fact derives from the Akkadian uz, meaning 'goat'. Other sources make it clear that the scapegoat ritual was done to propitiate Samael, another chief demon and fallen angel in Jewish tradition, whose name means 'poison of God'. Yet it is Azazel who is singled out in connection with Seir, for of him it was said, 'His portion among the peoples is Esau, a people who live by the sword; and his portion among the animals is the goat.

Mount Seir would seem to have been the original location of the scapegoat ritual conducted by Aaron and perpetuated each year in the Jewish feast of Yom Kippur, the Day of Atonement. Moreover, there is clear evidence that rabbinical scholars in medieval times attempted to disassociate this archaic practice with any kind of sacrificial offering made to the god of Seir. That Aaron, Moses' brother and the high priest of the tribe of Levi, sacrificed the scapegoat on Mount Seir in the land of Edom, where Egyptian records speak of a location called 'Yahweh in the land of the Shasu', is very interesting indeed. Here then we might expect to find the roots behind the worship of Yahweh.

Yahweh, the Tetragrammaton, or ineffable name of God, was first revealed to Moses when in Midian, the land of the Midianites, long considered to be northwest Arabia. One day, whilst tending the flock of Jethro, his father-in-law, comes 'to the back of the wilderness' and upon 'the mountain of God, unto Horeb', which means 'mountain in the desert'. Here he witnesses an 'angel of the Lord' in the form of a burning bush of fire. Before Yahweh announced himself to Moses, the god of the Israelites was referred to only by epithets such as Adon, 'lord', or variations of El, the Canaanite name of God, such as El shaddai... Yahweh was considered to inhabit the mountain, or at least dwell in a shrine that had been placed on the mountain and erected by himself for himself. I interpret the previous text as the authors stating that God devised a way for himself to exist on Earth as a microcosm.

In the Book of Exodus we learn that the Pesah, of Passover, celebrates the night that Yahweh 'passed over' the homes of the Hebrews when he sought out and killed the Egyptian first born. We now know that the reason why the Egyptians were afflicted as opposed to the Hebrews; the reason seems to be that because the Egyptian first born slept on a raised platform just as most Americans do today, they were exposed to the toxic vapors while the Hebrews who slept on the floor escaped death much in the same way as those who crawl on their bellies to escape the dangers of smoke inhalation in a house fire.

The Pesah feast was a night celebration beginning at sunset, culminating at dawn and was conducted in the presence of the deity. Coinciding, 'the face of Yahweh' and the 'glory of Yahweh' are old titles identified only with that of the full moon. In addition to this, it is a fact that at Arabic, Jewish, and Samaritan festivals worship does not begin until after the setting of the Sun and the appearance of the new moon; again most likely stemming from the fact that the ancients travelled at night. Pesah is generally translated into English as 'Paschal', as in the 'Paschal Lamb', a symbol of the Passion in Christian Easter Celebration. But in Hebrew Pesah does not translate into 'pass(over', Pasah does; while Pesah means rather 'protection'. Almost as if they were speaking of protection from the sorrows of the afterlife by way of preparation for death.

There is much evidence to show that the Israelites were influenced by the veneration of the moon. Significance can be found in the fact that Abraham's followers were known as Basran Sira, 'moon-deficients'. Sounds similar to the derogatory terms used for 'pot-heads' doesn't it? Almost as a way to signify deficiency associated with shamanism. Which actually makes a lot of sense when we are told time and time again that the reason why shamanism was placed in a lock box and had the key thrown away was the fact that it was not conducive of a system where slaves work for their owners. They were considered renegade moon worshippers because the moon was seen as unclean by the Mandaeans; they say it as a sinister influence, who is described as the 'bringer about of deficiency', 'causing insubordination', and 'overthrower'. This all supports the idea that shamanism causes major problems for any group whose goal is suppression.

In Mandaean legend, Bahram (Abraham) was a Mandaean from Harran(Chaldean). He began worshipping Yurba, a sun spirit liken to Aten and identified with the Hebrew Adonai, who was commanded by Ruha, queen of darkness. He destroyed all the idols in the great temple and went forth into the desert, and with him went all the "unclean and leprous and those who were deficient and of these Basran Sira their descendants were unclean and deficient until the seventh generation." Which tells us that they carried on with their own ways for seven generations until they gave in and conformed and joined back with the rest of the population.

It was during the reign of David's son Solomon that the First Temple was built, making Jerusalem both the seat of royal power and the national place of worship of the Israelite god. Here, in the Holy of Holies, rested the Ark of the Covenant, the vessel in which the deity is said to have been transported from place to place. The kings of Israel were anointed, a religious act that established a special relationship with God, thus making them the 'Anointed ones of Yahweh'. During the ceremony the spirit of Yahweh entered the candidate, enabling the anointing process to proceed.

In c. 640 BC a man by the name of Josiah was anointed king of Judah. Unlike a number of his predecessors who had fallen into idolatry, he was a fanatical follower of Yahweh, and was said to have 'walked all the way of David his father, and turned not aside to the right, or to the left.' Josiah revived the worship of Yahweh as a national religion and attempted to exterminate all forms of idolatry, which had perverted the land for generations. Eventually the 'pagan' god of Seir was denigrated into a demon or devil called Azazel or Edom. The god of Seir was not a pagan deity at all, but an inversion of the Israelites' own perception of the worship of Yahweh. In other words, he was simply the forgotten form of Yahweh, yet one, it would seem, that the

Israelites and later Jews would come to see as blasphemous.

Dhushara's consort is remembered in Petra under her pre-Islamic Arab name of al-Uzza. It is likely that this name also derived from the Akkadian uz, meaning 'goat'. This was the chief animal sacrificed to the various forms of Venus throughout the Near East, where she was also known as Allat, Astarte, Atargatis, Ishtar and rabbat al-thill, 'mistress of the Herd'. In early Christian tradition Ishtar/Venus evolved into the Whore of Babylon... In addition to this, there seems to be a direct relationship between the worship of al-Uzza and the scapegoat that Aaron sent to Azazel on Mount Seir in order that the Israelites might atone for their sins.

In Crete a kid was early substituted for a human victim; in Thrace, a bull-calf; among the Aeolian worshippers of Poseidon, a foal; but in backward districts of Arcadia boys were still sacrificially eaten even in the Christian era. Miletos may be a native Cretan, or a transliteration of milteios, 'the colour of red lead'; and therefore a synonym for Phoenix. Hera's name, ussually taken to be a Greek word for 'lady', may represent an original Herwa ('protectress'). She is the pre-Hellenic Great Goddess. Hera's forced marriage to Zeus commemorates conquests of Crete and Mycenaean - that is to say Cretanized - Greece, and the overthrow of her supremacy in both countries.

Wace's allusion to the sculpture in the relieving triangle over the Lion Gate is also worth quoting. "Sir Arthur Evans has shewn the significance of the type of this relief, the Sacred Pillar with the guardian lions, and has given illustrations of parallel types. The column is the sacred pillar of strength and protection, and is an aniconic form of a deity . . . In this case . . . the sacred pillar possibly stands for the Great Mother Goddess . . . The placing of such a relief over the citadel of Mycenae probably meant that it was placed under the protection of the Great Mother, and that she was the establisher of Mycenae.

At Hera's orders the Titans seized Zeus's newly-born son Dionysus, They tore him into shreds and boiled the peices in a cauldron, while a pomegranate-tree sprouted from the soil where his blood had fallen. His grandmother Rhea rescues and reconstitutes him, then on Zeus's instructions, Hermes temporarily transformed Dionysus into a kid, and presented him to the nymphs of Heliconian Mount Nysa. They tended Dionysus in a cave, cosseted him, and fed him on honey. It was on Mount Nysa that Dionysus invented wine, for which he is chiefly celebrated.

The myth of Erechtheus and Eumolpus concerns the subjugation of Eleusis by Athens, and the Thraco-Libyan origin of the Eleusinian Mysteries. An Athenian cult of the orgiastic Bee-nymph of Midsummer also enters into the story, since Butes is associated in Greek myth with a bee cult on Mount Eryx; and his twin brother is the husband of the =Active Goddess ', the Queen-bee. The name of King Tegyrius of Thrace, whose kingdom Erechtheus's great-grandson inherited, makes a further association with bees: it means 'beehive coverer'. Athens was famous for its honey.

The God Indra in the Ramayana had similarly wooed a nymph in cuckoo disguise; and Zeus now borrowed Hera's scepter, which was surmounted with the cuckoo. Gold-leaf figurines of a naked Argive goddess holding cuckoos have been found at Mycenae; in the well-

known Cretan sarcophagus from Hagia Triada a cuckoo perches on a double-axe. The marital relations of Zeus and Hera reflect those of the barbarous Dorian Age, when women had been deprived of all their magical power, except that of prophecy, and come to be regarded as chattels... Zeus's violation of the Earth-goddess Rhea implies that the Zeus-worshipping Hellenes took over all agricultural and funerary ceremonies. She had forbidden him to marry, in the sense that hitherto monogamy had been unknown; women took whatever lovers they pleased. It took the Hellenes three hundred years before they forced monogamy on Hera's people.

Amaltheia's name, 'tender', shows her to have been a maiden-goddess; Io was an orgiastic nymph-goddess; Adrasteia means 'the Inescapable One', the oracular Crone of autumn. Together they formed the usual Moon-triad. The later Greeks identified Adrasteia with the pastoral goddess Nemesis, of the rain-making ash-tree, who had become a goddess of vengeance. Io was pictured at Argos as a white cow in heat - some Cretan coins from Praesus show Zeus suckled by her – but Amaltheia, who lived on 'Goat Hill', was always a she-goat; and Melisseus ('honey-man'), Adrasteia and Io's reputed father, is really their mother – Melissa, the goddess as Queen-bee, who annually killed her male consort. Diodorus Siculus and Callimachus both make bees feed the infant Zeus – Hymn to Zeus.   -Dan Russell

The care with which the Nag Hammadi texts were copied and bound indicates that they were canonical to the copyists. As Abbot Shenoute of Panopolis near Nag Hammadi put it about forty years later, to a group of 'kingless' Gnostics who worshipped the 'demiurge' at the nearby temple of Nuit using 'books full of abomination' and 'every kind of magic,' refusing to acknowledge Archbishop Cyril, Patriarch of Alexandria, as their 'illuminator': "I shall make you acknowledge ... the Archbishop Cyril, or else the sword will wipe out most of you, and moreover those of you who are spared will go into exile."

"In 601 AD, Gregory I issued a papal edict concerning pagan practices. This law is responsible for converting many of the pagan holy days, or Sabbaths, into Christian Holidays, as is the case with Samhain, Hallowmas or Halloween which is celebrated by the church as "All Saint's Day." It is apparent that a similar thing happened with the pagan solstice traditions along with the elements of the classic shamanic experience. In his edict, Pope Gregory attributed Satan with the physical features of the pagan horned god Pan - cloven hooves and a goat's head - thus literally creating a scapegoat. A scapegoat is defined as a person bearing the blame for the sins and shortcomings of others; which is exactly what we have done to the horned god and the fly agaric mushroom. We have sacrificed the symbols of the dark side in favor of the light and glorious immortal hero that exists in human form. It seems that Jesus bore the suffering for our sins while Satan continues to take the blame for them.

These pagan elements of death and resurrection, a horned god and an immortal hero, are obviously central to Christianity. Many researchers of mushrooms and religion have suggested that the early Christians were an evolved mystery cult that practiced psychedelic initiation using the fly agaric."

From 'Ancient Persia' by Josef Wiesehofer, "Here is a quotation of the first lines of a martyr's story from Adiabene:

In the thirty-seventh year of our persecution [under Shapur II in the fourth century] a cruel command was issued, and the mobads were given power over all Christians to torment them with tortures and pains and to kill them by stoning and execution. The good shepherds who did not hide during this persecution were accused by the servants of evil, they said to the judges: 'The Christians destroy our doctrine and teach people to serve only one god, not to pray to the sun, not to worship fire, to pollute water by hateful washing, not to marry, not to beget sons or daughters, not to take the field with the kings, not to kill, to butcher and eat animals without qualms, to bury the dead in the Earth and to say that God, not Satan, has created snakes, scorpions and all the vermin of the world. They also spoil many servants of the king and teach them magic, which they call writings.' When the evil judges heard this, they flew into a great rage that burnt in them like fire in wood."

John Allegro was on the original team of scholars that had access to the Dead Sea Scrolls, and his renegade book The Sacred Mushroom and the Cross posited that Jesus was actually only a metaphor for the fly agaric and the powers it bestowed upon the initiate. The book was widely rejected early on, but is continually being read and referenced as a wave of new scholarship puts this question to the test. A new wave of research from writers like Jim Arthur provide even more support for a long history of psychedelic initiation in western religion. Clark Heinrich's Magic Mushrooms in Alchemy and Religion also carefully argues that the early Christians were indeed employing the fly agaric to achieve direct experience with God, and that the tradition was kept alive in the west through secret societies that formed during the middle ages around ancient vocations like stone masonry and metallurgy. According to scholars like Heinrich and Arthur, these groups evolved the practice of Alchemy to protect the secret of entheogenic mushroom initiation from the authority of the church and their genocidal inquisitions."

At the seat of transformation and renewal, the tree has a feminine and maternal significance. We have seen from Ripley's Scrowle that the tree-numen is Melusina. In Pandora the trunk of the tree is crowned, naked woman holding a torch in each hand, with an eagle sitting in the branches on her head. On Hellenistic monuments Isis has the form of Melusina and one of her attributes is the torch. Other attributes are the vine and the palm. Leto and Mary both gave birth under a palm, and Maya at the birth of the Buddha was shaded by the holy tree. According to legend, Adam stood in the same relation to the tree of life as Buddha to the Bodhi tree. In the teachings of the Barbeliots, reports Irenaeus, the Autogenes finally created "the man perfect and true, whom they called Adamas. With him was created perfect knowledge."

"In the middle of the crown, just on her forehead, there was a smooth orb resembling a mirror, or rather a white refulgent light, which indicated that she was the moon. The Druids of Britain and Gaul had a deep knowledge concerning the mysteries of Isis and worshipped her under the symbol of the moon. The moon was chosen for Isis because of its dominion over water. The Druids considered the sun to be the father and the moon the mother of all things. By means of these symbols they worshipped Universal Nature. The Druids had a Madonna, or Virgin Mother, with a Child in her arms, who was sacred to their Mysteries; and their Sun God was resurrected at the time of the year corresponding to that at which modern Christians celebrate Easter.

Just as Madonna was shown with a child in her arms who was sacred to their Mysteries, so too in Catholicism do we see the Virgin Mary with Jesus who is so sacred to their Mysteries. And just as with these two examples you can also see the mythology represented with Isis and her son Horus displayed on the right. I postulate that the virgin mother is the Earth, from whose bosom springs forth the mushroom without the requirement of a seed; therefore our mother Earth was a virgin when she begot our savior, born only of God's semen the rain.

In the Ripley Scrowle the serpent of paradise dwells in the top of the tree in the shape of Melusina." This is combined with a motif that is not the least Biblical but is primitive and shamanistic: a man, presumably an adept, is halfway up the tree and meets Melusina, or Lilith, coming down from above.

The climbing of the magical tree is the heavenly journey of the shaman, during which he encounters his heavenly spouse. In medieval Christianity the shamanistic anima was transformed into Lilith, who according to tradition was Adams first wife.

Furthermore Russell states:

"Iahu, the Sumerian Exalted Dove, was the daughter of Tiamat, the primeval waters. As the renowned linguist Professor John Allegro, Secretary of the Dead Sea Scrolls Fund and one of the original translators of the scrolls, teaches, IA, in Sumerian, means 'juice' or 'strong water.' The root idea of U, according to its usage in words like 'copulate' and 'mount,' is 'fertility,' thus 'Iahu' means 'Juice of Fertility.' That is the name of an entheogen, the fruit of 'the menses of Eileithyia.' 'Ishtar,' the Akkadian-Babylonian name, is derived from the Sumerian USH-TAR, 'uterus' in Latin.

Tiamat became the Tehom of Genesis. 'Firmament' means 'what is spread out,' and is a reference to the body of Tiamat. Marduk is Yahweh to Tiamat's Tehom. Marduk, or his hero Gilgamesh, was craftily portrayed as a winged shaman bringing the herb is immortality from heaven to Earth, thus usurping the function of Tiamat's daughter Iahu, the Original Yahweh, the Exalted Dove. Gilgamesh brings magical opium poppies to Earth on a relief, from the palace of Ashurnasirpal II, c. 875 BC. Gilgamesh was the Babylonian Odysseus. The earliest representations we have of this ritual legend were carved on Sumerian stone, c.3000 BC, and fragments of it were found in numerous sites, including Megiddo, Amarna, Khattusha, all dating back to c.1400 BC. Gilgamesh's quest is specifically entheogenic, as is the quest of Eve in Genesis.

Water and spirit are often identical. Thus Hermolaus Barbarus says: "There is also a heavenly or divine water of the alchemists, which was known both to Democritus and to Hermes Trismegistus. Sometimes

they call it the divine water, and sometimes the Scythian Juice,
sometimes pneuma, that is spirit, of the nature of aether, and the
quintessence of things." "...whose anointed eyes could easily look upon
the secrets of the philosophers." Hence the title of the Philosopher's
stone must be related to the "round white stone" and furthermore to the
fish or Jesus Christ being the spiritual gold hidden inside the lead, the
mushroom being a poisonous ocean, Jesus being the fish one must catch
to utilize the possible greatness of the Aqua Nostra.

"In the aqua nostra of the alchemists, the concepts of water,
fire, and spirit coalesce as they do in religious usage.

The text says:

Isis the Prophetess to her son Horus:

"My child, you should go forth to battle against the faithless
Typhon (Set) for the sake of your father's kingdom, while I retire to
Hormanuthi, Egypt's city of the sacred art, where I sojourned for a
while. According to the circumstances of the time and the necessary
consequences of the movement of the spheres, it came to pass that a
certain one among the angels, dwelling in the first firmament, watch me
from above and wished to have intercourse with me. Quickly he
determined to bring this about. I did not yield, as I wished to inquire
into the preparation of the gold and silver. But when I demanded it of
him, he told me he was not permitted to speak of it, on account of the
supreme importance of the mysteries; but on the following day an
angel, Amnael, greater than he, would come, and he could give me the
solution of the problem. He also spoke of the sign of this angel- he bore
it on his head and would show me a small, unpitched vessel filled with
a translucent water. He would tell me the truth. On the following day, as

the sun was crossing the midpoint of its course, Amnael appeared, who was greater than the first angel, and, seized with the same desire, he did not hesitate, but hastened to where I was. But I was no less determined to inquire into the matter. She did not yield to him, and the angel revealed the secret, which she might pass only to her son Horus." Then follow a number of recipes which are of no interest here. (I however, believe they are of utmost importance, as are the recipes found in Plato's Timaeus.) The angel, as a winged or spiritual being, represents, like Mercurius, the volatile substance, the pneuma."

A text from Edfu says: *"I bring you the vessels with the god's limbs(Osiris' limbs) that you may drink of them; I refresh your heart that you may be satisfied." The god's limbs were the fourteen parts into which Osiris was divided. There are numerous references to the hidden, divine nature of the arcane substance in the alchemical texts. According to this ancient tradition, the water possessed the power of resuscitation; for it was Osiris, who rose from the dead. In the "Dictionary of Goldmaking," Osiris is the name for lead and sulphur, both of which are synonyms for the arcane substance. Thus lead, which was the principal name for the arcane substance for a long time, is called "the sealed tomb of Osiris, containing all the limbs of the god." According to legend, Set covered the coffin of Osiris with lead. Petasios tells us that the "sphere of the fire is restrained and enclosed by lead." Olympiodorus, who quotes this saying, remarks that Petasios added by way of explanation: "The lead is the water which issues from the masculine element." But the masculine element, he said, is the "sphere of fire."*

So there we have it, the "sphere of fire," is the Amanita

muscaria mushroom, whose juices are poisonous and deadly, worthless as lead. This is easy to realize especially considering the other terms of the Amanita, the "winged fiery serpent," and so on. Osiris is obviously the mushroom then, able to be used, however one must get passed its leathal attributes. Cadmus killed the serpent in the same sense as Apollo killed the Python at Delphi. The names of the Sown Men - Echion ('viper'); Udaeus ('of the Earth'); Chthonius ('of the soil'); Hyperenor ('man who comes up') and Pelorus ('serpent') - are characteristic of oracular heroes.

Chapter Five: Alchemical Redemption

"Let us move on to Mercurius, "He is feminine, spiritual, alive and life-giving. He is also called husband and wife, bridegroom and bride, or lover and beloved. His contrary natures are often called Mercurius ensu strictiori and sulphur, the former being feminine, Earth and Eve, and the later masculine, water, and Adam. In Dorn he is the "true hermaphroditic Adam, and in Khunrath he is "begotten of the hermaphroditic seed of the Macrocosm" as "an immmaculate birth from the hermaphroditic matter" (i.e., the prima materia)."   - C. Jung

"The prima materia is an oily water and is the philosophic stone, from which branches multiply into infinity," says Mylius. Here the stone is itself the tree and is understood as the "fiery substance" or as "oily water." As oil and water do not mix indicative of the dual nature of Mercurius. As a rule, the lapis is synthesized from the quaternity of the elements or from the ogdoad of elements plus qualities (cold/warm, moist/dry). Similarly Mercurius, known from ancient times as quadratus, is the arcane substance through whose transformation the lapis, or goal of the opus, is produced.

The spirit which dwells in the Nile stone is blatantly related to Mercurius.

Christ's tearing of the breast, the wound in his side, and his martyr's death are parallels of the alchemical mortificatio, dismemberment, flaying, etc., and pertain like these to the process of transformation mushroom is put through.

Many things in Paracelsus that would otherwise remain incomprehensible must be understood in terms of this tradition. In it are to be found the origins of practically the whole of his philosophy in so far as it is not Cabalistic. It is evident from his writings that he had a considerable knowledge of Hermetic literature. Like all medieval alchemists he seems not to have been aware of the true nature of alchemy, although the refusal of the Basel printer Conrad Waldkirch, at the end of the sixteenth century, to print the first part of Aurora consurgens (a treatise falsely ascribed to St. Thomas Aquinas) on account of its "blashphemous character" shows that the dubious nature of alchemy was apparent even to a layman. To me it seems certain that Paracelsus was completely naive in these matters and, intent only on the welfare of the sick, used alchemy primarily for its practical value regardless of its murky background. Consciously, alchemy for him meant a knowledge of the materia medica and a chemical procedure for preparing medicaments, above all the well-loved arcana, the secret remedies. Now we are told that the distillation had to come from the midst of the center, this correlates directly with something I once read concerning splitting the stalk down the center and then running your fingernail along the middle of the inside of the stalk of the Amanita muscaria. I believe this is what the Green Dragon is that Jesus used to bring people back to life. As it says, the 'Green Dragon' is a fundamental idea in alchemy. Paracelsus does not fail to point out to his reader that this fire is not the same as the fire in the furnace. This fire, he says, contains nothing more of the "Salamandrine Essence or Melusinian Ares," but is rather a "retorta distillatio from the midst of the center, beyond all coal fire." Dorn says in "Physica genesis," Theatr. chem., I (1659), p. 349; "Of the center there is no end, and no pen can rightly describe its power nor the infinite abyss of its mysteries."

"Sophists" take the symbolical names concretely and attempt to make the magistery out of the most unsuitable ingredients. They were obviously the chemists of those days, who, as a result of their concretistic misunderstanding, working with common materials, whereas the philosophers called their stone animate because, at the final operations, by virtue of the power of this most noble fiery mystery, a dark red liquid, like blood, sweats out drop by drop from their material and then from their vessel."

This remarkable text explains the tree as a metaphorical form of the arcane substance, a living thing that comes into existence according to its own laws, and grows, blossoms, and bears fruit like a plant. This plant is likened to the sponge, which grows in the depths of the sea and seems to have an affinity with the mandrake. More frequently the tree appears bearing flowers and fruit. The Arabian alchemist Abu'l Qasim (13th cent.) The four colours refer to the four elements that are combined in the opus. The quaternity as a symbol of wholeness means that the goal of the opus is the production of an all-embracing unity. The motif of the double quaternity , the ogdoad, is associated in shamanism with the world-tree: the cosmic tree with eight branches was planted simultaneously with the creation of the first shaman. The eight branches correspond to the eight great gods. Cassiodorus allegorizes Christ as a "tree cut down in his passion," a parallel to the pine tree of Attis. In the Arabic "Book of Ostanes" there is a description of the arcane substance, or the water, in its various forms, first white, then black, then red, and finally a combustible liquid or a fire which is struck from certain stones in Persia." - Alchemical Studies C. Jung

"There is in the sea a round fish, lacking bones and scales, and it has in itself a fatness, a wonder-working virtue, which if it be cooked on a slow fire until its fatness and moisture have wholly disappeared, and then be thoroughly cleansed, is steeped in sea water until it begins to shine...."

This is a description of the transformation process. The alchemical tetrasomia and its reduction to unity therefore has a long prehistory which reaches back far beyond the Pythagorean tetraktys into Egyptian antiquity. From all this we can see without difficulty that we are confronted with the archetype of a totality image divided into four. The resultant conceptions are always of a central nature, characterize divine figures, and carry over those qualities to the arcane substances of alchemy. The fourfold Mercurius is also the tree or its spiritus vegetativus.

The Hellenistic Hermes is on the one hand an all encompassing deity, as the above attributes show, but on the other hand, as Hermes Trismegistus, he is the arch-authority of the alchemists. The four forms of Hermes in Egyptian Hellenism are clearly derived from the four sons of Horus. A god with four faces is mentioned as early as the Pyramid Texts of the fourth and fifth dynasties. The faces obviously refer to the four quarters of heaven- that is, the god is all-seeing. Remember now how the arcane substance will allow one to see visions of the future, and all that ever was. Another aspect of the dual nature of Mercurius is his characterization as senex and puer. The figure of Hermes as an old man, attested by archaeology, brings him into direct relation with Saturn- a relationship which plays a considerable role in alechemy; a role seen here, "At the end of the process, says Paracelsus, a "physical lightning" will appear, the "lightning of Saturn" will separate from the lightning of Sol, and what appears in this lightning pertains "to longevity, to that undoubtedly great Iliaster." From De vita longa, Lib. IV, cap. IV: "There are more than a thousand species thereof... so that each microcosm may have its own special and even perfect conjuction, each, I say, its own perfect and peculiar virtue". Gen. 5: 23-24: "...and Enoch walked with God: and he was not; for God took him." According to the chronologist Scaliger, Enoch was responsible for the division of the year and was also considered a prefiguration of Christ, like Melchisedek.

The mysterious rose-coloured blood occurs in several other authors. In Khunrath, for instance, the "lion lured forth from the Saturnine mountain" had rose-coloured blood according to a book titled "Von hylealischen Chaos", p. 93; also p. 197. This lion, signifying "all and conquering all," corresponds to the totality of Zosimos. Khunrath further mentions (p. 276)...

"The costly Catholick Rosy-Coloured Blood and Aetheric Water that flows forth Azothically (For Azoth, concerning "The Spirit Mercurius") from the side of the innate Son of the Great World when opened by the power of the Art. Through the same alone, and by no other means, are Vegetable, Animal, and Mineral things, by the ablution of their impurities, raised to the highest Natural perfection, in accordance with Nature and by the Art... From this little salty fountain (mycelium) grows also the tree of the sun and moon, the red and white coral tree of our sea." Salt and sea-water signify in Khunrath among other things the maternal Sophia from whose breasts the filii Sapientiae, the philosophers, drink. As we have seen, the tree has a special connection with water, salt, and sea-water, and thus with the aqua permanens, the true arcanum of the adepts, one adept stating: With this red stone the philosophers exalted themselves above all others and foretold the future. They prophesied not only in general but also in particular."

"Spirit in alchemy almost invariably has a relation to water or to the radical moisture, a fact that may be explained simply by the empirical nature of the oldest form of "chemistry," namely the art of cooking. The steam arising from boiling water conveys the first vivid impression of "metasomatosis," the transformation of the corporeal into the incorporeal, into spirit or pneuma. The relation of spirit to water resides in the fact that the spirit is hidden in the water, like a fish. In the "Allegoriae super librum Turbae" this fish is described as "round" and endowed with "a wonder-working virtue." As is evident from the text, it represents the arcane substance. From the alchemical transformation, the text says, is produced a collyrium (eyewash) which will enable the philosopher to see the secrets better."

The prima materia, as the radical moisture, has to do with the soul because the latter is also moist by nature and is sometimes symbollized by dew. In this way the symbol of the vessel gets transferred to the soul. There is an excellent example of this in Caesarius of Heisterbach: the soul is a spiritual substance of spherical nature, like the globe of the moon, or like a glass vessel that is "furnished before and behind with eyes" and "sees the whole universe." This recalls the many-eyed dragon of alchemy and the snake vision of Ignatius Loyola. In this connection the remark of Mylius that the vessel causes "the whole firmament to rotate in its course," is obviously referring the 'Holy Grail' which I believe is the many-eyed dragon of alchemy, the vessel that Mylius refers to is the Amanita muscaria in its mature stages as it forms a cup you can literally drink out of. Cited in

Preuschen, Antilegomena, p. 129; Justin Martyr says: "As a fount of living water from God... this Christ gushed forth."

Zosimos says of the round and omega element: "It consists of two parts. It belongs to the seventh zone, that of Kronos..." Kronos is Saturn, who is regarded as the dark "counter-sun." Mercurius is the child of Saturn, and also that of the Sun and Moon. Saturn is the origin of Satan most definitely. One of the most common and most important of the arcana is the aqua permanens, of the Greeks. This, according to the unanimous testimony of both the ancient and the later alchemists, is an aspect of Mercurius, and of this divine water Zosimos says in his fragment: This is the great and divine mystery which is sought, for it is the whole. And from it is the whole and through the same is the whole. Two natures, one substance. But the one attracts the one, and the one rules the one. This is the silver water, male and female, which forever flees.... For it is not to be ruled. It is the whole in all things. And it has life and spirit and is destructive.

You will begin to notice more and more just how much the Amanita muscaria is alluded to as the Microcosm of the universe with the stars being the Macrocosm with life on Earth being the cosm. Carl Jung says, "Zosimos's "whole" is a microcosm, a reflection of the universe in the smallest particle of matter, and is therefore found in everything organic and inorganic."

"The philosopher is not the master of the stone, but rather its minister." 6:52-59 The flesh and blood of the Son of man, denote the Redeemer in the nature of man; Christ and him crucified, and the redemption wrought out by him, with all the precious benefits of redemption; pardon of sin, acceptance with God, the way to the throne of grace, the promises of the covenant, and eternal life. These are called the flesh and blood of Christ, because they are purchased by the breaking his body, and the shedding of his blood. Also, because they are meat and drink to our souls. Eating this flesh and drinking this blood mean believing in Christ. We partake of Christ and his benefits by faith. The soul that rightly knows its state and wants, finds whatever can calm the conscience, and promote true holiness, in the redeemer, God manifest in the flesh. Meditating upon the cross of Christ gives life to our repentance, love, and gratitude. We live by him, as our bodies live by our food. We live by him, as the members by the head, the branches by the root: because he lives we shall live also. -Matthew Henry's Concise Commentary

And he said, "Unless you eat my flesh and drink my blood, you will have no life in you." ALAS! The Ahnk is none other than the giver of everlasting LIFE!

In "Isis to Horus," the angel brings Isis a small vessel filled with translucent or "shining" water. Considering the alchemical nature of the treatise, we could take this water as the divine water of the art, since after the prima materia this is the real arcanum. I believe these attributes are akin to the light of wisdom or knowledge that the mushroom's juices contain. The myth of Danae, Perseus, and the ark seems related to that of Isis, Osiris, Set, and the Child Horus. In the earliest version, Proetus is Perseus's father, the Argive Osiris; Danae is his sister-wife, Isis; Perseus, the Child Horus; and Acrisius, the jealous Set who killed his twin Osiris and was taken vengeance on by Horus. The ark is the acacia-wood boat in which Isis and Horus searched the Delta for Osiris's body. A similar story occurs in one version of the

Semele myth. Perseus killed the monstrous Medusa with the help of winged sandals. (Red Bull gives you wings!)

A Greek colony planted at Chemmis apparently towards the end of the second millennium B.C., identified Perseus with the god Chem, whose hieroglyph was a winged bird and a solar disk; and Herodotus emphasized the connexion between Danae, Perseus's mother, and the Libyan invasion of Argos by the Danaans. The myth of Perseus and the mushroom is perhaps told to account for an icon showing a hero studying a mushroom. Fire, mistaken for Water, is spouting from it under a blazing sun. Here is tinder for his fire-wheel. Perseus fortified Midea, and founded Mycenae, so called because, when he was thirsty, a mushroom [mycos] sprang up, and provided him with a stream of water. The Cyclopes built the walls of both cities. Thus Spake Zarathustra (trans. Kaufmann), p. 176: .Lonely one, you are going the way to yourself. And your way leads past yourself and your seven devils... You must consume yourself in your own flame; how could you wish to become new unless you had first become ashes!" And in Ars Chemica, p. 237: "Our stone slays itself with its own dart"; and the role of the incineratio and the Phoenix among the alchemists. The devil is the Saturnine form of the anima mundi. These were known to alchemists since earliest times. Olympiodorus, for instance, says that in lead (Saturn) there is a shameless demon (the spiritus mercurii) who drives men mad. (Berthelot, Alchimistes grecs, II, iv, 43.)

On 'The Visions of Zosimos', Steeb goes on to say that when the celestial waters were animated by the spirit, they immediately fell into a circular rotation, from which arose the perfect spherical form of the anima mundi. The rotundum is therefore a bit of the world soul, and this may well have been the secret that was guarded by Zosimos. All these ideas refer expressly to Plato's Timaeus. In the Turba, Parmenides praises the water as follows: "O ye celestial natures, who at a sign from God multiply the natures of the truth! O mighty nature, who conquers the natures and causes the natures to rejoice and be glad! For she it is in particular, whom God has endowed with a power which the fire does not possess... She is herself the truth, all ye seekers of wisdom, for, liquefied with her substances, she brings about the highest of works." As an arcanum, the egg is a synonym for the water. It is also a synonym for the dragon (mercurial serpent) and hence for the water in the special sense of the microcosm or monad. This tells us that the rotundum is obviously referring to the egg which symbolizes the mushroom as being directly linked to the universe as an all encompassing microcosm created at the moment that all of creation came into existence.

Socrates in the Turba says much of the same: "O how this nature changes body into spirit!... She is the sharpest vinegar, which causes gold to become pure spirit." "Vinegar" is synonymous with "water," as the text shows, and also with the "red spirit." The Turba says of the latter: "From the compound that is transformed into red spirit arises the principle of the world," which again means the world soul. This is western shamanism in all its glory, think birthday suit; the Catholic church will feel mighty naked when this gets out. The "red spirit" is sometimes said to be simply a synonym for the moist soul of the prima materia, the radical moisture. Another synonym for the translucent fluid is "spiritual blood" which Ruska correlates with "fiery medicine." So much for the Holy Grail, now that we know it was simply the literal blood of Christ, the juices from the mushroom.

Chapter Six: What is in front of you?

Jesus said, "If you become my disciples and pay attention to my sayings, these stones will serve you. For there are five trees in Paradise for you; they do not change, summer or winter, and their leaves do not fall. Whoever knows them will not taste death."

"The Church burned enormous amounts of literature. In 391 Christians burned down one of the world's greatest libraries in Alexandria, said to have housed 700,000 rolls. All the books of the Gnostic Basilides, Porphyry's 36 volumes, papyrus rolls of 27 schools of the Mysteries, and 270,000 ancient documents gathered by Ptolemy Philadelphus were burned. Ancient academies of learning were closed. Education for anyone outside of the Church came to an end. - Helen Ellerbe

(The Dark Side of Christian History)

The Vatican has miles of documents secretly hidden away underneath its premises. Some might argue at first, "Well how are they secretly hidden if people know they are there." I used the word secretly specifically because although we know the documents are there, we are not permitted to look at them. In fact, quite a few documents have been denied translation because some people had certain ideas of what was contained in the documents.

Amanita muscaria in the left hand, and a Cannabis sativa stick/Hemp rod, in the right denoting "KING" with the divine right to rule. The sacred rite with the plants of truth on the nuptial couch is reference to the sacred marriage of the mystery religions, the hieros gamos, as mentioned in the Essene Thanksgiving Hymn.

Here are some other pictures that point towards the importants of the Trinity's symbolic meaning. I submit that they point towards the drugs that made the King "KING".

The Archangel Michael or Melchizedek; one Hebrew high
priest or Zadok, an Essene composite of the archangel Michael... he is
pictured holding a Rod and Sphere[of fire?].

Above: Hera Queen of the Heavens, and wife of Zeus, painted by Abraham Wuchters. Zeus is holding the thunderbolt (Amanita muscaria/orb) in his left hand, Hera is holding the scepter (Cannabis Sativa) in her right hand. It would seem fitting to know that the mushrooms were thought to grow after lightning struck the ground, and that this belief was held until just recently with the invention of the microscope when we could then see the spores.

I opened up a book I recently purchased at a yard sale of 'The Boy Pharaoh' by Noel Streatfield, where on page 32 they have the above image. I realized that the head on the staff that I was attempting to prove was hemp, was none other than the Dog 'Anubis'. This makes perfect sense when we remember that Anubis is the God who helped Isis put the body parts of Osiris back together. I've always known that Cannabis was mixed with the Amanita muscaria to reduce the naseau caused from the ingestion of the ibotenic acid that hadn't fully absolved.

In many passages the phrase "benai adom," the "sons of Adam," is used to denote men of Israel. Remember that Israel was the name of Jacob, the younger brother who was making red stew who later became the father of the Hebrew tribes. Israel is simply Isis-Ra-Elohim, as Nabisco is National-Biscuit-Company. One does not find the phrase "benai eesh" when being used to describe the sons of Adam; they are different from the sons of evolutionary man. I believe the "sons of Adam" specifically refer to the "sons of the red mushroom." The royal colors were an attempt to identify themselves with that original Adom, specially created man, the original Jesus who died for our sins only to rise again.

GENESIS 6

1 Now it came to pass, when men began to multiply on the face of the Earth, and daughters were born to them
2 that the sons of God saw the daughters of men, that they were beautiful; and they took wives for themselves of all whom they chose.
3 And the LORD said, "My Spirit shall not strive with man forever, for he is indeed flesh; yet his days shall be one hundred and twenty years."
4 There were giants on the Earth in those days, and also afterward, when the sons of God came in to the daughters of men and they bore children to them. Those were the mighty men who were of old, men of renown. (NKJV)

The first, and oldest, belief is that "the sons of God" were fallen angels who fornicated with human women, producing giant offspring called nephilim. This view was widely held in the world of the 1st century CE, and was supported by Flavius Josephus, Philo, Eusebius and many of the "Ante-Nicene Fathers," including Justin Martyr, Clement of Alexandria, Origen, Tertullian, Irenaeus, Athenagoras and Commodianus.

The second view is one which was first suggested by Julius Africanus and later advocated by Saint Augustine, the Catholic Bishop of Hippo. Augustine rejected the concept of the fallen host having committed fornication with women. In his early 5th century book The City of God, he promoted the theory that "the sons of God" simply referred to the genealogical line of Seth, who were committed to preserving the true worship of God. He interpreted Genesis 6 to mean that the male offspring of Adam through Seth were "the sons of God," and the female offspring of Adam through Cain were "the daughters of men." He wrote that the problem was that the family of Seth had interbred with the family of Cain, intermingling the bloodlines and corrupting the pure religion. This view has become the dominant one among most modern biblical scholars.

The third view is that "the sons of God" were the sons of pre-Flood rulers or magistrates. This view took hold in rabbinic Judaism after Rabbi Simeon ben Yochai pronounced a curse in the 2nd century CE upon those Jews who believed the common teaching that the angels were responsible for the nephilim. This interpretation was advocated by two of the most respected Jewish sages of the Middle Ages, Rabbi Shlomo Yitzchaki (Rashi) and Rabbi Moshe ben Nachman

(Nachmanides), and became the standard explanation of rabbinic Judaism. However, it is not widely accepted by modern scholars.

The Book of Enoch (also called I Enoch) is a collection of pseudepigraphic writings by various authors which dates to the 1st or 2nd century BCE. This book was well-known by the early church; in fact, Jude, the brother of Jesus, quoted Enoch 1:9 in verses 14 and 15 of his epistle. Obviously Jude felt that the Book of Enoch he had access to in the 1st century was trustworthy. This work, which survived to our day against great odds, deals extensively with the fall of the angels. It was viewed favorably by some early "Christian" writers also (Irenaeus, Clement of Alexandria, and others). However, it was never universally accepted as inspired Scripture.

Below is a selection from the Book of Enoch which records the sin of the angelic "watchers":

ENOCH 6

1 And it came to pass when the children of men had multiplied that in those days were born unto

2 them beautiful and comely daughters. And the angels, the children of the heaven, saw and lusted after them, and said to one another: 'Come, let us choose us wives from among the children of men

3 and beget us children.' And Semjaza, who was their leader, said unto them: 'I fear ye will not

4 indeed agree to do this deed, and I alone shall have to pay the penalty of a great sin.' And they all answered him and said: 'Let us all swear an oath, and all bind ourselves by mutual imprecations

5 not to abandon this plan but to do this thing.' Then sware they all together and bound themselves

6 by mutual imprecations upon it. And they were in all two hundred; who descended in the days of Jared on the summit of Mount Hermon

JUBILEES 5

1 And it came to pass when the children of men began to multiply on the face of the Earth and daughters were born unto them, that the angels of God saw them on a certain year of this jubilee, that they were beautiful to look upon; and they took themselves wives of all whom they

2 chose, and they bare unto them sons and they were giants. And lawlessness increased on the Earth and all flesh corrupted its way, alike men and cattle and beasts and birds and everything that walks on the Earth – all of them corrupted their ways and their orders, and they began to devour each other, and lawlessness increased on the Earth and every imagination of the thoughts of all men

3 (was) thus evil continually...

Nicholas de Vere, in his book 'The Origin of The Dragon Lords of the Rings', adds: "The Dionysic Rites were cannibalistic and vampiric and echo the era of the cannibalism and vampirism of the (Titanic) era of the sons of the Nephilim."

The International Standard Bible Encyclopedia on possible origins of this Hebrew word: nephilim The etymology of nephilim is uncertain, the following explanations have been advanced with mixed reception. First, it may derive from the niphal of the verb pala, meaning "be extraordinary," i.e., "extraordinary men." Second, it may be derived from the verb napal, "fall," in one of the following senses: (1) the "fallen ones" – from heaven, i.e., supernatural beings; (2) morally "fallen men"; (3) "those who fall upon," in the sense of invaders or hostile, violent men; (4) "those who fell by" the sword (cf. Ezk. 32:20f.); (5) "unnaturally begotten men" or bastards (from cf. nepel, "abortion" or "miscarriage"). (pp. 518-519, vol. 3) First, let's look at all of the Old Testament references to "sons of God." This phrase is translated from the Hebrew beney 'elohim, beney ha'elohim, and beney 'elim: GENESIS 6:1 When men began to increase on Earth and daughters were born to them,

2 the divine beings [beney ha'elohim] saw how beautiful the daughters of men were and took wives from among those that pleased them.

3 The LORD said, "My breath shall not abide in man forever, since he too is flesh; let the days allowed him be one hundred and twenty years."

4 It was then, and later too, that the Nephilim appeared on Earth when the divine beings [beney ha'elohim] cohabited with the daughters of men, who bore them offspring. They were the heroes of old, the men of renown. (Tanakh, the new Jewish Publication Society translation according to the traditional Hebrew text)

DEUTERONOMY 32:8 When the Most High gave to the nations their inheritance, when He separated the sons of men, He fixed the bounds of the peoples according to the number of the sons of God [beney 'elohim]. (RSV)

Let us for a moment look at that last passage from Deuteronomy, "When the Most high gave to the nations their inheritance", so in other words when the Ruler of the Empire was dispersing the goods of the empire, "He separated the sons of men, He fixed the bounds of the peoples according to the number of the sons of God [beney 'elohim]" meaning the bounty in which the people were allotted was based off of how many members of the land belonged to the Royal Leaders group the Sons of the Elohim.

What is the Elohim considered to be then? It is also known as those who from the Heavens came to Earth, or those who from Heaven to Earth came. The spores of mushrooms are made of chitin, the hardest naturally-made substance on Earth. Some scientists suspect that mushroom spores are capable of space travel; a few even believe that some fungi found on Earth originally came from outer space, which is saying that Mushroom spores would be the only thing on the planet that can exist in space and still multiply on the face of the Earth.

Elohim, would be "He who is the object of fear or reverence." The meaning of Elohim is further investigated by the fact that it is used to describe the spirit of the dead prophet Samuel, raised by Saul in 1 Samuel 28:13. The witch of Endor tells Saul that she sees 'gods' (elohim) coming up out of the Earth; this seems to indicate that the term was indeed used simply to mean something like 'divine beings' in ancient Israel.

The elohim coming up from out of the Earth could very well be the mana that is mentioned in the Bible. This would mean that the Sons of the Elohim were the Sons of the Mushroom. This is beginning to make more and more sense isn't it, the Sons of God were a group of people who worshipped the mushroom, kept their knowledge secret and sacred. They were the high priests, rulers of the known world, whose members did not interbreed with common women, only those women who were of worthy social recognition. It makes sense that the rulers known as the "beney 'elohim" disgraced their people by interbreeding with the common folk or the daughters of men.

Remembering back now that nephilim means bastard children, unnaturally begotten children, is it a stretch to say that according to their laws it was unnatural for a member of social importance to copulate with women based solely on their beauty and not wealth or family stature? Then it also makes sense that of these nephilim rose great leaders or giants among men with many followers leading to great tyranny. Not to mention that the mushrooms are seemingly unnaturally begotten as well.

Let's go back to 1 Enoch to see what these fallen angels did that affected the human race enormously:

1 ENOCH 8 1 And Azazel taught men to make swords, and knives, and shields, and breastplates, and made known to them the metals of the Earth and the art of working them, and bracelets, and ornaments, and the use of antimony, and the beautifying of the eyelids, and all kinds of costly stones, and all

2 coloring tinctures. And there arose much godlessness, and they committed fornication, and they

3 were led astray, and became corrupt in all their ways. Semjaza taught enchantments, and root-cuttings, Armaros the resolving of enchantments, Baraqijal (taught) astrology, Kokabel the constellations, Ezeqeel the knowledge of the clouds, Araqiel the signs of the Earth, Shamsiel the signs of the sun, and Sariel the course of the moon. And as men perished, they cried, and their cry went up to heaven...

I would say that people from a foreign land came and taught their ways to another culture, that it was against their rules to intermingle as to not degrade their own lineage of their race of peoples, and that the beauty of the women was too great to heed or suppress their desires and thus the Sons of Elohim took unto themselves daughters of mere men! Out of these bastard children arose great leaders, men of renown, giants of their time!

Chapter Seven: It's All God, Some's Just a Little Better

"From the outset Israeli culture was inherently multi-ethnic, containing former Egyptian slaves of all colors and backgrounds. The great genius of the Israelite approach to religio-social organization was to do what native cultures of the great slave states were incapable of doing. Israel freed itself from the thrall of totemic magic, losing, of course, important points of contact with its shamanic roots, if not hidden on purpose as we will soon find out later. The books Israel produced, Torah (Outpouring), Nevi'im (Prophets), and Ketuvim (writings), The Holy Bible, though varied, have became the most influential writings of the ancient world, eventually supplanting Homer and Hesiod as the basic texts." -Dan Russell

The book, The Phoenicians, says quite clearly, "testimonies from the Old Testament were much fuller, especially when it came to relations with Tyre, and to Solomon's times, when the Tyrian king, Hiram I, had the temple of Solomon built in Jerusalem. Later, relations between the kings of Israel and the kings of Tyre extended to religious matters, such as the influence on Israel exerted by Phoenician polytheism."

Russell Cont... "Naturally, as a beleaguered group in a state of almost constant warfare, wild shamanic nonconformity was frowned upon, in favor of effective group action. There was, and is, a powerful ethos of conformity in Israel's mandatory monotheism that Rome was eventually to find quite useful when it became 'the true Isreal.' Moses' brother Aaron, the kohen, saw two of his sons struck dead for celebrating the Lord with 'illicit fire', and Judges attributes Israel's defeat in battle to serving 'the baalim and the ashtaroth.' Jeremiah promises divine vengeance upon those who worship the popular 'Queen of Heaven,'and archeology proves that she was indeed popular. As Gordon and Patai point out, if we had no Bible, but only the evidence of Israeli archeology, we would conclude that Israelite religion, until the destruction of the Temple in 586 BC, was mainly the worship of Astarte, Asherah."

"Greek philosophers distinguished Promethean man from the imperfect Earth-born creation, part of which was destroyed by Zeus, and the rest washed away in the Deucalionian Flood. The Gilgamesh tablets are late and equivocal; there the 'Bright Mother of the Hollow' is credited with having formed everything and the principal theme is a revolt against her matriarchal order, described as one of utter confusion, by the gods of the new patriarchal order. Marduk, the Babylonian city-god, eventually defeats the goddess in the person of Tiamat the Sea-serpent; and it is then brazenly announced that he, not anyone else, created herbs, lands, rivers, beasts, birds, and mankind. This Marduk was an upstart godling whose claim to have defeated Tiamat and created the world had previously been made by the god Bel - Bel being a masculine form of Belili, the Sumerian Mother-goddess."

The transition from matriarchy to patriarchy seems to have come about in Mesopotamia, as elsewhere, through the revolt of the Queen's consort to whom she had deputed executive power by allowing him to adopt her name, robes, and sacred instruments. Some deny that Prometheus created men, or that any man sprang from a serpent's teeth. They say that Earth bore them spontaneously, as the best of her fruits. These men were the so-called golden race, subjects of Cronus, who lived without cares or labour, eating only acorns, wild fruit, and honey that dripped from the trees, drinking the milk of sheep and goats, never growing old, dancing, and laughing much; death, to them, was no more terrible than sleep. They are all gone now, but their spirits survive as genii of happy music retreats, givers of good fortune, and upholders of justice.

Though the myth of the Golden Age derives eventually from a tradition of tribal subservience to the Bee-goddess, the savagery of her reign in pre-agricultural times had been forgotten by Hesiod's day, and all that remained was an idealistic conviction that men had once lived in harmony together like bees. Serpent-tailed Boreas, the North Wind, was another name for the demiurge Ophion who danced with Eurynome, or Oreithyia, Goddess of Creation, and impregnated her. The North Wind, which bent the pines, was held to fertilize women, animals, and plants."

-The Greek Myths by Robert Graves

".... if the agaric should say to a man 'You will melt away soon' then the man would see his legs, arms, and body melt away, and he would say, "Oh! Why have I eaten of the agaric? Now I am gone!"

On Christmas Eve, for instance, Chris Bennett notes that the people of Poland and Lithuania serve semieniatka, a soup made from hemp seeds. The Poles and Lithuanians believe that on the night before Christmas the spirits of the dead visit their families and the soup is for the souls of the dead. A similar ritual takes place in Latvia and in the Ukraine on Three Kings Day. Yet another custom carried out in deference to the dead in Western Europe was the throwing of hemp seeds onto a blazing fire during harvest time as an offering to the dead - a custom that originated with the Scythians and has seemingly been passed on from generation to generation for over 2500 years."

Of Which That Follows, I Cannot Track the Author, My apologies. 821AD A learned professor, student of European and Slavic (Russian) folklore, and poet, Reverend Clement Moore, gathered together all the elements of European lore, deities and folk-characters, added them to the descriptions of his fellow countrymen at the Historical Society and Washington Irving, and created a poem which was to become the gospel of Santa Claus for every writer and artist for a century to come. Called 'A visit from St. Nicholas ' or 'The night before Christmas' But he did this poem for his children, and when it was published by a friend, Moore did not allow his name to be associated with it until 1837 There were subsequently many different publications, each illustrated according to the characteristics dictated by the poem, published from 1823 onwards, and while Thomas Nast has been attributed with being the first to illustrate Santa Claus, this assumption has long since been corrected by a vast number of earlier illustrations being found. 1863AD Thomas Nast did a political cartoon of Santa entitled 'Santa in Camp', for Harpers Weekly Journal. Dressed in Stars and Stripes Santa had joined the civil war on the side of General Grant in the North . Perhaps he could have also appeared (being Santa, and strictly neutral) dressed in rebel gray for the South, but if so it was a private drawing as the South did not have the publishing resources of the North. 1864-1886AD Thomas Nast continued to draw Santa Claus every year, and became known as THE Santa Claus artist of the mid-1900's. Meanwhile Britain was importing illustrations and cards depicting Santa Claus from Germany. He was called Father Christmas by the English, following the 17th. changes, and that name stuck. He was usually represented as a tall, almost aesthetic character, saintly and stern rather than the 'Jolly Elf' character being portrayed by the Americans. 1860's The English custom of a visit from Father Christmas was revived and established as the character visiting on Christmas Eve and leaving gifts for children in their stockings. Images, dolls and artwork from Germany helped to strengthen this custom. The Germanic images showed him as a saint, in bishops robes, as a winterman in furs, as a saintly old man, often seen in the company of the Holy Child, and as a giftbringer in robes of every colour from brown, white, green blue to golds, pinks and red. Even in this latter guise, his countenance was serious more often than jolly, though laughing Santas did appear. These were usually those which were influenced by the American imagery, and intended for export to the USA. 1870's SantaClaus began to put in appearances in Department stores in the USA and Canada. 1873 Louis Prang of Boston published the first American Christmas Card. His images showed Santa Claus much in the same tradition as the earlier American images, but with a softer, gentler look. More the saintly old gent than the jolly old elf. 1890's Father Christmas began to appear in English Stores. 1922AD Norman Rockwell created a perfect blend of saintly and jolly when he created Santa for the Saturday Evening Post.1931AD Coca Cola began their major promotion using Santa to promote their drink. Their artist, Haddon Sundblom created Santa in his own image! It is the Coca-Cola Santa which springs to mind now as the traditional Santa. 1948AD Department Stores in Britain increased the thrill of their Santa Grotto with train rides, sleigh rides, trip to the moon and elaborate animated scenes.c. mid-1950's English Father Christmas slowly gives way to American Santa Claus. 1980's European traditions of Giftbringers begin to give way to Santa Claus. Spains's Three Kings ,

Italy's Befana, and Sweden's Tomte in particular have all given way to Santa as the anticipated Giftbringer, sometimes even as an additional giftbringer.

Now think back and remember how in 1821AD A learned professor, student of European and Slavic [Russian] folklore, and poet, Reverend Clement Moore made Santa. Shortly after Thomas Nast drew Santa. Many say that Coca-Cola claims to take responsibility for the colors and image that comes in the mind of millions when they think of Santa, however it's obvious that that is a false claim just for sales because any informed person knows that Thomas Nast is responsible for the image of Santa. Not Coca-Cola, they just failed to acknowledge that they simply copied the image right from Nast.

So let's think for a moment about the image of Santa. The original Christmas Ornaments, some of the oldest that can be found today were red and white mushrooms. Santa is also in red and white, as were the bishops in Bill and Ted's Excellent Adventure, and the church liasons in The Search for the Holy Grail. Indeed these people wore red and white throughout history. In fact they resembled Santa more so than the St. Nick that Santa is supposed to personify. How ironic is that, the fact that little boys and girls for decades have been sitting on the laps of old men in malls that more appropriately personify church elders like cardinals and bishops, especially with this church scandal that recently passed.

But more strenuously I must point out the connection between the red and white Amanita muscaria mushroom. Like I mentioned, the very first original Christmas ornaments were red and white Amanita muscaria mushrooms. There is a very good reason for this! And it will explain a lot of the mysteries that lay behind just where this learned author got his material for Santa Claus.

Let's start with the chimney; in Siberia where the mushroom grows up high in the mountains under stunted trees, the native families live in round huts covered with straw or whatever material available. Often snowing, the huge amount of snowfall coupled with the wind and snow drifts often blocked access to the front door. The only access into and out of the home was thru a little hatch in the roof of the hut. This is why in the Americanized version Santa enters through the chimney.

Why do Santa's reindeer fly? They fly because the reindeer love Amanita muscaria mushrooms and they would eat them right up as soon as confronted with one on the ground. The shaman that would come around to collect the mushrooms was often said to have to fight off the reindeer in order to throw them in the sack before they were all taken. Thus they would metaphorically take flight after consuming the magic mushrooms.

Why do we have stocking-stuffers? Because the Amanita muscaria mushroom is poisonous when wet. The shaman would usually hang them stalk down in the limbs of the tree, and come around the next day on his same route and collect them, oops I gave away why we have ornaments... but if he was in a hurry or he had a lot in particular he would hang a filled loose-knit stocking over the fire place to dry large quantities.

It's all starting to come together now isn't? Just wait though it's about to get a whole lot more interesting. This mushroom, when it's born, arrives in a bulbous egg-like shape, as it grows it bust out of its white membrane and the veil remnants that are left behind are the white spots on the red skin of the mushroom. Easter is the family role playing the symbolized mushroom hunt; where the whole family used to run around with baskets collecting as many magic mushrooms as possible.

Rabbits have long been associated with fertility and the mushroom, in fact rabbits are known for eating mushrooms that cause their droppings to become large and yellow. These droppings can grow so large they rupture the flesh and cause bleeding. This is how the 'Easter Bunny' can lay the eggs that we search for, the 'eggs' they leave behind were originally mushrooms when they went in. Our church leaders that controlled the flow of society through their church teachings were indeed very manipulative and sly as foxes; but we must be wise as serpents!

Russian Dolls symbolize the fractals one sees visually after ingesting the mushroom, as do all Russian dolls, these are just more blatant in their connection with Santa myth and lore. I was recently at a friend's house where their parents had on display a set of Russian doll with various images of Jesus Christ portrayed on them. I couldn't help but think about how much different my reality was from their own. To me that was quite a display considering how Jesus the mushroom was exactly what those dolls were portraying, and no Christian displaying those would know that. But seeing those Santa dolls next to the Jesus dolls really makes quite more sense when you think about the fact that Santa was a shaman of Siberia, and Jesus was a shaman for his people. And both are portrayed as the mushroom by being painted on the Russian dolls.

Some Synonymous names for this Mushroom through history are: (Thanks to Chris Bennett)

1. Soma (Hindu plant God.)

2. Amrita (Buddhist Magical Sacrament.)

3. Ambrosia (Greek Food of the Gods.)

4. The Holy Grail (Grail like Shape, Vessel containing the blood of the God.)

5. Fruit of the Tree of life (The main Body (mycelium) growing underground in Symbiotic relationship with the pine tree.)

6. The Golden Fleece (The magical Properties tell all.)

7. The Fountain of Youth (How many did Ponce De Leon kick over while searching?)

8. Haoma (Islamic Sacrament.. Hmm Why all the Fighting?)

9. Manna (Two kinds don't look in the Ark or You are dead!)

10. Bread of Life (Yes, it's the Loaf of Bliss!)

11. Fountain of living Waters (It is Alive and it is 90% water!)

12. Hidden Manna (Hidden until you find it!)

13. The Cosmic Egg (What are we really Mimicking at Easter?? The Mushroom hunt?)

14. The Prima Materia (Alchemy's mystery substance!)

15. The Water of Life (Pressed Juices of Soma Ancient Stuff!)

16. The Flesh of the God (Sure does Resemble Flesh!)

17. The Fruit of Knowledge (Open your eyes!)

18. The Flesh of Jesus (Take and Eat..!)

As you can see from images throughout history, the four leaf clover in past times was often associated hand in hand with the Amanita muscaria mushroom!

So Santa is a Shaman who merrily goes along picking mushrooms in lower mountains of Siberia, dries them, and delivers them as gifts to his fellow villagers. He symbolizes this as clothing himself in red and white among other things we have discussed. These shamans of the North typically lived in semi-nomadic communities that were in close relationship with reindeer. After studying the behavior of these reindeer for his book Soma, R.G. Wasson concluded that "Reindeer have a passion for mushrooms and especially for the fly agaric, on which they inebriate themselves." His claim is supported by others stating that the reindeer prance around wildly after eating of the agaric. Not only the shaman, but the reindeer also eat the mushroom and apparently feel its magic. Here we have a situation that very closely resembles that of Santa Claus, the old wise man who lives at the north pole among a heard of flying reindeer.

Regarding Alchemical Texts:

"Many treatises define Mercurius simply as fire. He is ignis elementaris, noster naturalis ignis certissimus, which again indicates his "philosophic" nature. The aqua mercurialis is even a divine fire. This fire is "highly vaporous." Indeed, Mercurius is really the only fire in the whole procedure. He is an "invisible fire, working in secret." One text says that the "heart" of Mercurius is at the North Pole and that he is like a fire." – Jung

The names of Santa's Reindeer that most of us know by heart come to us from the same poem 'Twas the night before Christmas, yet they too seem to have associations with mushrooms, both their growth cycle as well as their role in the classic shamanic experience. For example, Donder and Blitzen, which come from the Germanic words for thunder and lightning, may have actually originated in the ancient belief that mushrooms appeared wherever lightning struck the Earth.

This was considered truth until relatively recently, with the advent of the microscope in modern times, when humans discovered that mushrooms propagate by releasing spores from their gills. In the case of the fly agaric, soaking rains are necessary for a mushroom to emerge out of the ground, hence the association with thunder and lightning. Furthermore, the fly agaric grows in a mycorrhizal relationship with certain trees like birch, fir and pine. The mushroom is actually the fruiting body of an underground network of threadlike fibers called mycelium which grow among the roots of "Christmas trees".

"We have already seen how reindeer have an appetite for the fly agaric, and their names seem to corroborate this fact. For example, Dasher, Dancer and Prancer can be seen merely as slick nicknames expressing the athleticism of Santa's showoff reindeer, or these names can be seen to refer to the effects that the fly agaric has upon not only the reindeer, but the shaman as well. Claims of running extremely fast or for very long distances, and trance-dancing for hours on end are not uncommon in reports made by people who have eaten of the agaric.

The word comet refers to a heavenly body in flight. In my view, the flying reindeer named Comet becomes a kind of code word for astral travel under the influence of entheogenic mushrooms. One common sensation associated with the classic shamanic experience is that of leaving one's body and taking flight. A comet is also celestial, the heavens are its domain, and as we will see time and again, entheogenic mushrooms like the fly agaric can be seen as keys which unlock the doors to heaven.

Cupid is the name of another reindeer on Santa's team. How should this ancient Roman god of love who is normally associated with

Valentines Day (another red and white holiday) come to be the appellation of a flying Christmas reindeer? Again, I submit that the best way to make sense of it is through the experience of mushroom entheogens, particularly the fly agaric. Cupid is the messenger of Eros, god of love. Entheogenic mushrooms like the fly agaric have the potential to awaken feelings of love that range from the profoundly spiritual kind of boundless love, to rapture or ecstasy, to the very Earthy sensual love that includes the erotic, which in this context also becomes sacred. Clark Heinrich describes the blissful sensuality inherent in the fly agaric experience, "It is as if every pore of the body were a sexual organ in orgasm, and I am not overstating things." The notion of ecstasy is a repeated theme in mushroom shamanism and Christmas alike.

And finally we come to Vixen, the one distinctly feminine reindeer. Today the word vixen means a spiteful or quarrelsome woman, but earlier it meant simply fox-lady. The word sounds a lot like wiccan which of course is associated with witches and witchcraft. Wiccan originally means "to bend," referring to a witch as one who bends or shapes reality and perception. It is not unsafe to speculate on the meaning of vixen in this context as a shape shifter or witch. The "fox-lady" represents women's magic in the very same way Santa represents men's magic. Mushrooms like the fly agaric can allow one to attain shamanic powers such as magical flight and shape shifting. These reindeer names refer to the transpersonal states of mind accessed by witches and sorcerers, initiates and shamans throughout time immemorial."   - Unknown Internet Author

The names of Santa's reindeer, like many of the symbols of Christmas, come to us from mushroom shamanism through the filters of ancient paganism, religion, secret societies, underground cults, and folklore. For example, the Norse god Thor also flew through the sky in a magical chariot pulled by horses or reindeer in some versions of the story. And many people are probably still under the impression that the Christian St. Nicholas who resembles Santa Claus in his benevolent wisdom and powers of immortality is in fact the beginning of the story. But when we dig just a little bit deeper we find an older blueprint that is actually much more accessible than one could ever possibly imagine.

The classic shamanic experience is global and timeless. It has analogues in states of consciousness referred to as mystical, visionary, numinous, transpersonal or peak. Inherent in the shaman's journey we find symbols and themes that are similar and relevant to Santa Claus and Christmas, especially the themes of immortality and shape shifting. On his journey, the shaman typically undergoes a transformation that involves the very real experience of his own death. Subsequently, he has access to transpersonal states of being and realms beyond the living. For example this Koryak shaman from northern Siberia speaking about the effects of the fly agaric shows the inherent theme of death and resurrection in the experience:

".... if the agaric should say to a man 'You will melt away soon' then the man would see his legs, arms, and body melt away, and he would say, "Oh! Why have I eaten of the agaric? Now I am gone!" Or should the agaric say 'Go to The One-on-High,' the man would go to The-One-on-High. The latter would put him on the palm of his hand, and twist him like a thread, so that his bones would crack, and the entire world would twirl around.'Oh I am dead!' that man would say. 'Why have I eaten the agaric?' But when he came to, he would eat it again, because sometimes it is pleasant and cheerful. Besides, the agaric would tell everyman, even if he were not a shaman, what ailed him when he was sick, or explain a dream to him, or show him the upper world or the underground world, or foretell what would happen to him."

This candid report tells of the veracity of the death experience under the influence of the Amanita muscaria and helps to define some of the contents of a shamanic or mystical experience, particularly death and rebirth, healing, knowledge and access to the upper and lower worlds. To make further sense of the connection of chimney sweeps to the fly agaric I offer this poem by the 17th century visionary, William Blake. Through it we can get a deeper look into the mystery of the top hat wearing chimney-sweeps and their hidden knowledge.

William Blake from Songs of Innocence:
"And so he was quiet, and that very night
As Tom was a-sleeping, he had such a sight! That thousands of sweepers, Dick, Joe, Ned & Jack,
Were all of them locked up in coffins of black. And by came an Angel who had a bright key,
And he'd open the coffins and set them all free; Then down a green plain, leaping, laughing they run,
And wash in the river, and shine in the sun. Then naked and white, all their bags left behind,
They rise upon clouds and sport in the wind; And the Angel told Tom, if he'd been a good boy,
He'd have God for his father, and he'd never want joy. And so Tom awoke; and we rose in the dark,
And got with our bags and our brushes to work. Tho' the morning was

cold, Tom was happy and warm;

So if all do their duty they need not fear harm."

"This poem offers another clue to the hidden meaning of mushrooms, chimney sweeps and Christmas in its underlying theme of death, resurrection and enlightenment. One can also detect a possible hidden reference to the fly agaric mushroom as well. Blake begins this poem with the line "and so he was quiet" which describes a prerequisite condition for a visionary state – inner silence. Then Tom, as the chimney-sweep is called, has not a dream but a vision ("such a sight!") while he was sleeping. Sleeping in this case could actually refer to a meditative state either naturally or chemically induced, especially after the initial proclamation that he was quiet first and foremost. Also, the fly agaric sometimes induces a temporary unconscious sleep-like state in those who ingest it.

In his vision Tom sees "thousands" of chimney-sweeps, himself included, sealed in black coffins which is clearly symbolic of death. Then an Angel appears to Tom with a "bright key" to set them free, clearly an allegory of resurrection. This can also be read, in my opinion, as a reference to the fly agaric with its bright red color and its potential for unlocking the doors to eternity. Which is exactly what happens next in our poem when Tom and the other chimney-sweeps frolic and play in an Edenic garden before they miraculously ascend to the heavens, "rise upon clouds and sport in the wind." Then the angel told Tom, if he was a good boy he'd have God as a father which sounds strikingly similar to Christ, the son of God. Finally, when Tom has to get back to the daily grind of his Earthly existence, and although they "arose in the dark" and the "morning was cold" we are assured that the wisdom of the experience is still with him as he was "happy and warm" and without fear.

Here we have an allegorical descriptive of a classic psychedelic journey: first silence, then death followed by a visitation from an angel, or celestial "other" with the "bright key" to paradise culminating in an out of body ascension. These are universal ingredients found in reports of shamanic voyages and psychedelic experiences throughout time and across the globe. This visionary poem suggests that the chimney sweep craft is a vital link from the middle ages to modernity that perhaps carries with it the knowledge of mushroom shamanism during the dark ages of theocratic rule.

It appears to me that chimney sweeps may represent one such vocation that evolved with ancient secrets like mushroom initiation. Gordon Wasson birthed the field of ethnomycology with his research on the Amanita muscaria mushroom. His 1968 book Soma attempted to identify the Vedic god of intoxication as the fly agaric. While Wasson discusses mushrooms and reindeer extensively, he does not approach the subject of Santa Claus or Christmas directly, except for very briefly in the following point about chimney sweeps: "The red mushroom with white spots appears frequently on greeting cards to convey good wishes and a seasonal message of happy augury, A noteworthy thing: this attribute of happy augury belonging to the [fly agaric mushroom] is regarded by chimney-sweeps as peculiarly theirs." It seems that something much more than a friendly association of good luck charms is going on here. Santa Claus is a chimney slider, which is to say, the chimney sweeps know his secrets and vice versa. Perhaps the chimney sweep profession represents a secret society that held onto the shaman's ancient secret of the fly agaric mushroom in fear of persecution from the church.

The three ominous colors, red, white and black resonate throughout time with Santa's magic. And while many writers have noted the mysterious power these colors have on the Western mind, few have connected them with the fly agaric. For example, in his book The Winter Solstice: the Sacred Traditions of Christmas by John Matthews, the author suggests that fire and snow account for the power that red and white hold over us: "...The symbolism of red fire in the white desert of Winter is a vital image. Is it stretching the point too far to see an echo of this in the red and white costume and white beard of [Santa Claus]? Certainly the importance of these colors throughout the northern world is beyond question." Matthews talks of the shaman's flying reindeer and his journey through the heavens in search of the gifts of fire and prophecy, but never attempts to explain how the shaman might come to accomplish this supernatural feat.

Robert Bly writes about the symbolic significance of the colors red, white and black in his book about men, Iron John. "The fairy tale hero or heroine, whether in Russian, German, or Finnish tales, who chances to see a drop of red blood fall from a black raven into the white snow, sinks immediately into a yogic trance. That suggests the vast power red, black, and white have or have had over human consciousness up through the Middle Ages." Bly uses the story Iron John to explore men's issues and finds a thread of truth and hope in recovering men's power by getting in touch with the archetypal wild man through reclaiming male initiation. He offers a vast array of potential interpretations for the symbolism of red, white and black.

Among them are sexual symbols; white for semen and red for menstrual blood. Alternatively, birth, maturity and death are offered for the meaning of white, red and black, respectively. But ultimately Bly settles on the idea that the three colors represent a developmental sequence, a spiritual maturation process, phases of initiation. Red for youth, white for adulthood and black for old age, for example. Yet the red and white mushroom is never considered. As we have seen, entheogenic mushrooms have been a vital component in spiritual initiation for humans throughout time.

It seems that many Santa Claus scholars are either frustratingly overlooking the fly agaric, for one reason or another, or they are choosing to omit it. In her book Santa, The Last of the Wild Men, Phyllis Siefker connects Santa Claus back to a 50,000-year-old tradition of shamanism through the persistence of wild-man plays into the 20th century in Europe intended to celebrate the Winter Solstice. The consistent theme found in these plays is the sacrificial death and resurrection of the village wild-man for the well being of the community. In the play, the horned wild-man is hunted and killed for his affiliation with the young maiden of the village, only to be miraculously reborn again. Siefker notes the similarity in the themes of these plays and those found in the classic shamanic experience, as we have seen time and again, "there are similarities too striking to ignore or chalk up to coincidence... We are asking questions to which no firm answers exist, yet the overwhelming similarities of these rituals, and the astonishing pervasiveness of their spread throughout Europe, imply an origin so ancient and so deeply rooted, it may have predated any European civilization, indigenous or imported." That this scholar may have missed a vital component in the answer to her question is evidence of how big of a secret the fly agaric really is."

"The power of shape shifting along with the experience of one's own death and resurrection are two key aspects of the classic shamanic experience. These two themes are essential to understanding the iconography of Christmas and will help to reveal a deep connection between Santa Claus and mushrooms. The question arises, if in fact Santa is connected to mushroom shamanism as it appears, then where and how has this knowledge remained hidden for so long? This is a simple question with a rather complex answer that involves the demonization and criminalization of mushroom shamanism over time. The story of how this practice has become outlawed in the west is ironically intertwined with how Santa Claus and our entire Christmas tradition came to be. A closer look at the iconography of this holiday will help to reveal this connection.

Bears are usually included in images of Christmastime. They are among the earliest symbols of death and resurrection. Bear skins were worn by shamans to connote the transformation by man into totem animal. Bear skulls have been found among early human burial remains, suggesting a strong belief in the bear's power of rebirth, or immortality. The bear disappears in winter into a subterranean trance-like existence called hibernation until springtime, when he reemerges from the Earth. This perennial custom has a powerful analogue to the sun in winter who all but disappears by the solstice in the most northerly latitudes only to return again for another year. The bear has persisted as a powerful symbol of strength, renewal, protection and healing all over the world and his relationship to the winter solstice has secured him a place of prominence in Shamanism as well as in Christmas lore.

Bears are directly connected to the Amanita muscaria through the Germanic word Berserk. The term Berserker is commonly known to refer to a class of Viking warrior who reportedly ate the fly agaric for added strength, courage and ferocity before going into battle. The term today still carries connotations of rage or craziness. Berserk translates literally as 'bear shirt,' however, which would have originally meant something like wild man or shaman, who was either literally hairy like a bear or figuratively donned the skins of a bear in ceremony. The shaman resembles the bear in ceremony because he is in communication with the bear in the natural world as well as in the spirit realm. He looks like the bear because he has become the bear and attained its powers of rebirth. Here we see two common themes of shamanism clearly represented; shape shifting on the one hand, and death and resurrection on the other.

These two themes are played out in the otherworldly dimensions of the shaman's journey, which include the lower and upper worlds. The lower world is underground and commonly accessed by a tunnel or a hole in the Earth. It is populated by guardian animals who protect and heal. The upper world is associated with the sky and is accessed by such means as a sacred tree, or ladder that reaches into heaven. The upper world is celestial in nature and is associated with knowledge, ancestral wisdom, immortality and eternity. It is often times populated by spirit beings that guide and teach and going there is sometimes accompanied by feelings of ecstasy or religious rapture.

The image of the sacred tree whose roots lead underground, to the lower world, and whose branches stretch to heaven, is the likely origin of the tradition of the Christmas tree. For the shaman, the Sacred Tree forms an axis from the perspective of everyday experience in the center, surrounded by the four sacred directions, the upper world above, and the lower world below. As we have seen, entheogenic mushrooms like the Amanita muscaria – which literally grow under the "sacred tree" - provide initiation into the otherworldly dimensions of the shaman.

It is clear that both the upper and the lower worlds are realms of healing for the shaman, an experience of the eternal can be as valuable as merging with an animal ancestor. Perhaps it is simplistic to assert that these two realms, the upper and the lower worlds are responsible for the division of reality into heaven and hell in our collective mind and later enforced by religion. However it seems that is basically what happened. As paganism was replaced by monotheistic religions in the west like Judaism and Christianity, inter-species communication, shape shifting and psychedelic mushrooms were relegated to the hell realm, while religious ecstasy, ascension, and eternity were deemed righteous. The horned gods, like Pan, were demonized and made into the devil, Satan, while the divine hero whose seed form we find in Osiris and Dionysus is the kind we in the West chose to officially worship instead, as in the case of Jesus. Understanding this split in human consciousness - the division between heaven and hell - is essential to the story of Santa and the mushroom. This subtle division also includes the inherent sexism that has plagued human history as the western conceptualization of nature as Mother Earth is clearly of the lower world and God or Father Sky (time) is king of the heavens. We in the west have come to generally favor all things associated with the upper world which tend to be expressions of the masculine principle and mistrust, fear and thus demonize the feminine aspects of our identity. Our great challenge collectively as well as individually, is to balance these two aspects within ourselves.

One way to approach an understanding of this duality is through the very names we bestow to symbols such as the Devil and Santa Claus. There is an obvious anagram between Satan and Santa, providing a clue that perhaps they are two aspects of the same being, alter egos, twins, as it were. When we consider the "nick" names of each archetype, an even more intimate relationship is revealed. For example, Satan is often referred to as Old Nick, whereas Santa Claus is called Saint Nick. Both "Nicks" account for the two extremes of the archetypal shamanic experience. Over time we have subconsciously assigned the parts of our hero's journey that we dislike and cannot accept to the underworld. The wild side of shamanism includes animal transformations, herbalism and Earthy sexuality. These are attributes we ascribe to the devil and witches. The parts of the story that we can accept or identify with, such as immortality, religious rapture, wisdom, and prosperity we associate with heaven, Jesus, saints and Santa Claus. Old Nick represents the dark side whereas Saint Nick defines the light."

-James Bursenos

Chapter Eight: Buddha was said to hop around on one leg when he was born. This is his footprint.

McKenna concedes that the original sacraments in any religion were no doubt entheogenic in nature whether cannabis, cactus, mushroom or some other rare flower. Sadly, humans have replaced the nectar of the gods with cheap substitutes. McKenna names alcohol, tobacco, sugar, coffee, tea, heroin, cocaine and television all as substitutes for the psychedelic experience, calling them drugs of a dominator style society. He reminds us that the slave trade and colonialism were developed and sustained by these goods which offer only temporary stimulation and frustrating addictions. Sugar, caffeine, alcohol and tobacco have been culturally supported whereas the sacramental use of entheogenic mushrooms are still demonized and outlawed.

With the concealment of the mushroom, and forcing the pagans "underground" they were no longer able to keep their fertility festivals alive. Mushrooms are dangerous to those who hold the power and influence today, Jesus mentioned in the Bible those who keep the sacred rites a secret and do not partake in the rituals themselves. It is clear to me that plant and mushroom entheogens were once the birth rite of every human being.

Gradually, they became controlled and substituted with cheaper and more addictive substances. Terence McKenna discusses this process thoroughly in his revolutionary book, Food of the Gods. He writes, "Hierarchically imposed religion and, later, hierarchically dispensed scientific knowledge were substituted for any sort of direct experience of the mind behind nature."

If the entheogenic plant had not spilled its vital blood for us, we would have no way to be saved, no door to bring us into heaven. Here we have a foundation for the only religious freedom that matters: the freedom to eat God's flesh as he has admonished, and drink his Life-giving blood. If we are permitted to "worship" but only in such a way that we do not consume God's true entheogenic flesh and drink his true entheogenic blood, then there simply is no possibility of any true worship. Worshipping God *is* consuming entheogenic flesh and blood, hence the two sons that were struck dead for celebrating God with illicit fire; there is no reason to worship and there is no worship, without consuming this.

"They" wiped the history of Western shamanism clear off the grid of time; or tried to at least. When an American hears the word Shamanism He/She automatically thinks of lesser evolved, pre-civilized animal spirit religion. The truth of the matter was laid forth in this book, shamanism is all that there is as far as religion goes, all that has happened is that those in power have hidden this fact. I have tried to show that there was at least one common element that was pervasive throughout the entire globe, the Amanita muscaria. From every continent upon which mankind resides, the Amanita muscaria was there; in the middle of it.

Here we have a shaman's sacramental letters, not pistis, 'faith,' but a very active participation mystique, a "psychedelic experience," and the consequent originality and matristic ideology that was anathema to the Bishops of Lyon and Rome. Valentinus understood Iasius, as he called him, as the "fruit of the knowledge of the father" - an hermaphroditic combination of Adam, Eve, the serpent and the fruit - offering an original gift, not original sin. Some Gnostics, notably the famous Alexandrian teacher Basilides, insisted that sex was to be enjoyed without any sense of guilt, as a sort of baptism in the material world which prepared one for the next level. Basilides was a teacher of Valentinus, the most popular and influential Christian Gnostic. In several Gnostic creeds, Mary Magdalene was secretly educated by Jesus in the arts of love. Among the Valentinians women were completely equal, prophesying, healing and officiating right alongside the men.

"Then they anoint the initiate with balsam, for they say that this ointment is a type of the sweet fragrance which is above all things... 'redeeming' the dying up to the moment of death, pouring oil and water on their heads, or the ointment mentioned above mixed with water, and with the invocations mentioned above, that they may not be grasped or seen by the principalities and powers, and that their inner man may ascend even above the invisible things.... And they claim that he who says this will avoid and escape the powers..." What is clearly being described here is a pre-death ritual, belief that by keeping the soul in this state of constant free-mind that the mind will be spared the burdens that the soul endures during the process of death."

The myth is that 108 snails sacrificed themselves one day while noticing Buddha was meditating deeply under the warmth of the sun, they decided to protect him from the Sun's harsh rays and in doing so dried up sacrificing themselves for the Buddha. Do you notice how these Buddhist figures with their 108 snails on top of their heads resemble the early stages of the mushroom?

Snails are often seen climbing around on the tops of these Amanitas most likely eating them as a snack. One-hundred eight is a very important number to Buddhism, it equates to 9 which is a sacred number in Chaldaen numerology.

I know that some folks will no doubt attempt to discredit this book by claiming that the author fantasizes about mushrooms every second of every day and that I see mushrooms everywhere within everything. However that is just simply not the case, in fact it took me quite a while to attune or hone my mushroom connection detection skills. Where previously I would have only figured out the link after reading over twice, with greater overall knowledge comes easier identification of the familiar; thus promptly realizing the similarities. During the last month of the development of this book a friend of a friend of mine gave me another book to read. He sort of brushed it off as an interesting book that says pretty much what I was trying to say, but that he found other areas of religious studies more satisfying.

The book was 'The Greek Myths: Volume One' and the following is the forward by the author of the book Robert Graves:

Since revising The Greek Myths in 1958, I have had second thoughts about the drunken god Dionysus, about the Centaurs with their contradictory reputations for wisdom and misdemeanor, and about the nature of divine ambrosia and nectar. These subjects are closely related, because the Centaurs worshipped Dionysus, whose wild autumnal feast was called 'the Ambrosia'. I no longer believe that when his Maenads ran raging around the countryside, tearing animals or children in pieces and boasted afterwards of travelling to India and back, they had intoxicated themselves solely on wine or ivyale. The evidence, summarized in my What Food the Centaurs Ate, suggests that Satyrs(goat-totem tribesmen), Centaurs (horse-totem tribesmen), and their Maenad womenfolk, used these brews to wash down mouthfuls of a far stronger drug: namely a raw mushroom, Amanita muscaria, which induces hallucinations, senseless rioting, prophetic sight, erotic energy, and remarkable muscular strength. Some hours of this ecstasy are followed by complete inertia; a phenomenon that would account for the story of how Lycurgus, armed only with an ox-goad, routed Dionysus's drunken army of Maenads and Satyrs after its victorious return from India.

On an Etruscan mirror the Amanita muscaria is engraved at Ixion's feet; he was a Thessalian hero who feasted on ambrosia among the gods. Several myths are consistent with my theory that his descendants, the Centaurs, ate this mushroom; and, according to some historians, it was later employed by the Norse 'berserks' to give them reckless power in battle. I now believe that 'ambrosia' and 'nectar' were intoxicant mushrooms: certainly the Amanita muscaria; but perhaps others, too, especially a small, slender dung-mushroom named panaeolus papilionaceus, which induces harmless and most enjoyable hallucinations. A mushroom not unlike it appears on an Attic vase between the hooves of Nessus the Centaur. The 'gods' for whom, in the myths, ambrosia and nectar were reserved, will have been sacred queens and kings of the pre-Classical era. King Tantalus's crime was that he broke the taboo by inviting commoners to share his ambrosia.

Sacred queenships and kingships lapsed in Greece; ambrosia then became, it seems, the secret element of the Eleusinian, Orphic and other Mysteries associated with Dionysus. At all events, the participants swore to keep silence about what they ate or drank, saw unforgettable visions, and were promised immortality. The 'ambrosia' awarded to winners of the Olympic footrace when victory no longer conferred the sacred kingship on them was clearly a substitute: a mixture of foods that the initial letters of which, as I show in What food the Centaurs Ate, spelled out the Greek word 'mushroom'. Recipes quoted by Classical authors for nectar, and for cecyon, the mint-flavoured drink taken by Demeter at Eleusis, likewise spell out 'mushroom'.

I have myself eaten the hallucigenic mushroom, psilocybe, a divine ambrosia in immemorial use among the Masatec Indians of Oaxaca Province, Mexico; heard the priestess invoke Tlaloc, the Mushroom-god, and seen transcendental visions. Thus I wholeheartedly agree with R. Gordon Wasson, the American discoverer of this ancient rite, that European ideas of heaven and hell may well have derived from similar mysteries. Tlaloc was engendered by lightning; so was Dionysus; and in Greek folklore, as in Masatec, so are all mushrooms – proverbially called 'food of the gods' in both languages. Tlaloc wore a serpent-crown; so did Dionysus. Tlaloc had an underwater retreat; so did Dionysus. The Maenads' savage custom of tearing off their victims' heads may refer allegorically to tearing off the sacred mushroom's head – since in Mexico its stalk is never eaten. We read that Perseus, a sacred King of Argos, converted to Dionysus worship, named Mycenae after a toadstool which he found growing on the site, and which gave forth a stream of water. Tlaloc's emblem was a toad; so was that of Argos; and from the mouth of Tlaloc's toad in the Tepentitla fresco issues a stream of water. Yet at what epoch were the European and Central American cultures in contact?

These theories call for further research, and I have therefore not incorporated my findings in the text of the present edition. Any expert help in solving the problem would be greatly appreciated.

R.G.

Deya, Majorca Spain, 1960

Now upon receiving the book I immediately set upon skimming through it while highlighting any major key aspects of the book that were applicable to my studies. In doing so I learned an invaluable lesson being that one should always read a book from cover to cover. Reason being is that when I sat down to go over the few notes I took I decided to read the foreword of the book and I instantly encountered a flood of emotions.

At first I was purely shocked that a half century ago a man summarized much of my book in his foreword, after which I dreaded that in fifty years no one will have heard of my book just as I had never heard of this one. Finally I came to grips with the idea that my book was very different, it had a different soul simply because I poured my own soul into it. At least now I am no longer worried about pouring my heart and soul into something irrelevant.

In 1955, Graves published The Greek Myths, containing translations and interpretations. His translations are well respected and continue to dominate the English-language market for mythography, whereas some of his unconventional interpretations and etymologies are dismissed by classicists but have provoked more research into the topics he raised. Graves dismissed the reactions of classical scholars, arguing that by definition they lacked the poetic capacity to forensically examine mythology. In 1961 he became professor of poetry at Oxford, a post he held until 1966.   - Wikipedia

                    http://en.wikipedia.org/wiki/Robert_Graves

I suggest reading the entire page.

Here is a TIME article that anyone can read on the internet.

Monday, May. 16, 1960

Myths, Muses & Mushrooms

Robert Graves's mother used to warn him against becoming "like people who feed birds in public gardens, and usually have two or three perched on their heads." But Mother scarcely foresaw the strange-feathered notions that would roost inside Grave's head. Out of this intellectual aviary fly de-crested myths, twice-tweaked Bible tales, a poetic cockatoo called the White Goddess, and great whooping cranes of scholarly controversy. As a man who travels "full-speed in the wilder regions of my own, some say crazy, head," Graves ranges airily from poetry to poltergeists, from mushrooms to Majorca (his expatriate home). Though the form changes—essay, lecture, story, poem—the wryly cantankerous wit and charm remain the same.

The Little Foxes. Graves is one of the few men of letters who can talk shop, for example, without putting up the shutters of boredom or obscurity. What does a good poet do? He captures the sound of his own voice talking, says Graves, a natural voice and "not the one in which we try to curry favor with children at a party, or with an election crowd, or with a traffic cop." To show what happens when a poet merely apes passing fashions. Graves does a parody of a Japanese haiku called "The Loving Parents":

In his more eccentric vein. Graves maintains that neither Benedict Arnold nor Judas were traitors. Sample argument: "A dishonest treasurer, as Judas is represented as being, would not have sold out at that petty price." The title piece of Food for Centaurs is a superlative action shot of Graves in the fine, frenzied throes of a theory.

By some recondite detective work, he reaches the conclusion that the centaurs' food was mushrooms. It was a very special scarlet-capped European mushroom, known as the fly-amanite. According to Graves, this mushroom is fiery to the taste, imparts extraordinary muscular strength and creates overpowering sexual desire.

In antiquity, says Graves, some mushrooms went by the nickname of "little foxes." This sets the stage for one of his brazenly assured and highly speculative exegeses of Biblical texts. It is highly unlikely, argues Graves, that Samson caught 300 real foxes, set their tails afire and turned them loose to burn the cornfields of the Philistines. What he probably did was to arm 300 soldiers with flaming torches and inflame the men with the mushroom wonder drug.

When the lovely Shulamite in The Song of Solomon cries "Take us the foxes, the little foxes, that spoil the vines; for our vines have tender grapes!", she is asking for the fiery aphrodisiac, according to Graves, to be washed down with flagons of wine.

Love Is the Object. For a man who can read a lot into a mushroom, Graves remains singularly incurious about the ancient sites that have spurred so much of his writing. At 62, the author of I, Claudius finally did go to Rome for the first time. In Centaurs he candidly admits that he has yet to see Athens, Corinth, Mycenae, Constantinople and Jerusalem. "The truth is, I dislike sight-seeing," says Graves. Most modern cities fill him with despair and still another theory: "I believe that closer research into human fatigue-reactions would show that perfectly straight lines and perfectly flat surfaces, perfect circles, and exact right angles, induce between them much of the mental illness for which functionally-built modern cities are notorious."

As for the afterworld, all suggested versions strike Graves as equally and disastrously dull, be it "the Moslem Heaven of sherbet, tiled baths and complaisant houris" or "the Norse Valhalla with its endless battles and mead-orgies" or "the Judaeo-Christian Heaven of golden temples, where only a chaste sodality reigns." They all lack love, says Graves (two marriages, seven living children), and he adds of himself: "I have never not been in love since boyhood."

MUSHROOMS AND RELIGION

By Robert Graves

"The profound importance of mushrooms in primitive religion had remained undetected until some twenty years ago, when Mr. R. Gordon Wasson, an American banker, and his Russian-born wife Valentina first called attention to it. The new science of ethnomycology, meaning the attitudes of different races to mushrooms, began with the Wassons' puzzling over the division of Europe into two distinct camps: mycophobes (nations traditionally afraid of mushrooms) and mycophages (nations addicted to eating them). The mycophages of Europe are found in Spain, Southern France, the Balearics, Bavaria, the Balkans and Russia. Russians are the greediest mushroom eaters and recognize over ninety varieties of edible ones.

Until recently we English ate only the white field mushroom psalliotis campestris, except in the Midlands where blewets were sold in the markets. But as a boy in North Wales I found even the field mushroom avoided as poisonous.

My mother had spent her childhood in Bavaria where mushrooms grew profusely in my grandfather's pine woods, and when taken there for holidays as a child I soon learned to distinguish seven or eight edible varieties and bring them back to the kitchen for dinner. Home in Wales, I came across some of these same mushrooms growing in the woods and brought them back to eat; but my mother astonished me by shouting: 'Throw those toadstools away at once! Yes, I know that they look like the ones we ate last week at Lauzforn, but here they are deadly poison. You had better wash your hands!' Whether she really believed this-her view seemed borrowed from my mycophobic Irish father-or whether she had to take this attitude because the cook would give notice the moment they were brought into the kitchen, I have never decided.

The existence of so many million unreasoning mycophobes throughout Northern Europe and North America -though, to be sure, some of them now dare to accept cooked mushrooms from abroad, neatly bottled-reminds me of another curious taboo in force among the ancient Greeks. They were forbidden to eat any bright red food, such as lobsters, crabs, prawns and wild strawberries (which had no name because regarded as poisonous). The Hebrew word syeg, meaning a 'hedge', explains both these taboos. To protect the Biblical ban on, for example, buying or selling on the holy Sabbath, the Jews of Jesus's day had put a protective 'hedge' around the Fourth Commandment by forbidding anyone to carry coins on his person from Friday evening until Saturday evening. And the truth is that mushrooms had once been regarded as holy and reserved for priests, kings and other privileged people; therefore to prevent the unprivileged from eating a sacred mushroom; a general syeg was put on mushroom-eating and reinforced by treating all mushrooms as poisonous. However, as already mentioned, an unexplained relaxation of the taboo in England allowed the eating of white field mushrooms, though the most deadly European mushroom of all, the amanita phalloides, with which Nero's stepfather the Emperor Claudius had been poisoned, was equally white and has often been mistaken for it.

It is therefore reasonable to guess that the sacred mushroom originally protected by these taboos grew in forests, not in fields, and was scarlet; and that the taboo explains the diabolic or disgusting names given even to highly edible other mushrooms.

But why was the scarlet mushroom (which can be easily identified with the white-spotted one now favored by red-coated gnomes in suburban gardens and also associated with Father Christmas's reindeer and decorated tree) held sacred? This spectacular mushroom, incorrectly rumored to be deadly poison, grows by the millions all over the British Isles, but only in birch forests. A simple answer is that this was the magical mushroom, on which sat the caterpillar smoking his hookah, that Alice found growing in Wonderland. Lewis Carroll had read about its properties not long before he published the book; they included the same hallucinations about height-'curiouser and curiouser'-from which Alice suffered after nibbling it.

This mushroom, named Amanita muscaria-popularly 'fly agaric'-has now been proved by Gordon Wasson's detailed examination of the Vedic hymns (written in Sanskrit about the time of the Trojan War), to have been the Food of the Gods. It is there named 'Soma'. That it is also 'Ambrosia' and 'Nectar' (both these words mean 'immortal') which were famous as the food and drink of the Greek Olympian gods, I had myself shown some twelve years previously. Two early Greek poets, Sappho and Alcman, had preserved the ancient tradition of Ambrosia as a drink, not a food. This was because the juice of the mushroom-which lost its virtue when cooked-was squeezed out of it between boards, then mixed with milk or curds; and the pulp was thrown away. According to these Vedic hymns, Agni, the god of mystic illumination and holy fire, who was also expressly identified with Soma, had been created when the Father God Indra threw a lightning bolt at the Earth.

Dionysus (Bacchus), the Greek god of mystic illumination, was similarly born when his father the God Zeus (Jove) threw a lightning bolt at the Earth Goddess Semele; the bolt killed Semele but her child was saved and sewn up in his father's thigh, whence he was later granted a second birth. Dionysus is said to have eventually conducted his mother to Heaven where she changed her name to Thyone, meaning 'Queen of the Maenads' (or raging women) and presided over Dionysus's ecstatic October festival, called The Ambrosia. October was the mushroom season.

The effect of the Amanita muscaria taken without other intoxicants is to give the taker the most delightful hallucinations, if he is in a state of grace, but horrible nightmares otherwise. Fortified, however, with beer and the juice of yellow ivy it would send Greek men and women raging mad. A mixture of Amanita muscaria with whisky has long been used as a celebratory drink by successful salmon-poachers in Scotland. It is called a 'Cathy', in honor of Catherine the Great of Russia who is said to have been partial to it.

The pre-Classical priests of Dionysus, a god now known to have been active in Mycenean times, seem to have claimed the sole rights in the scarlet mushroom, the memory of which they had brought from their original homes in Central Asia and which is not found growing south of the fortieth parallel, except at a great height and always in birch groves. The Vedic priests of Agni seem to have imported their supply from the birch-groves of the high Himalayas. Throughout the world mushrooms were believed to be begotten only by lightning.

That Dionysus was Ambrosia, as his Indian counterpart Agni was Soma, is proved by the legend of his birth from Zeus's thigh. The Vedic hymns make it clear that the priests of Indra and Agni used the two different ways of taking Soma still found among the Palaeo-Siberians called Korjaks, and also in a small Mongol enclave of Afghanistan. The first was a simple drinking of the juice pressed from the mushrooms between boards and mixed with milk or curds. The hallucinogenic indoles it contained entered the stomach; but a great many more entered the kidneys and were later discharged with the urine.

Clean-minded Classical scholars have until now shut their eyes to the possibility that the Vedic hymnwriter may have meant exactly what he said with 'the great gods piss out together the lovely Soma'. Yet it has been known for at least two centuries that the Korjaks do so after drinking the mushroom juice, and that their friends strain the urine through wool and, after drinking it, enjoy the same ecstasies. And this, of course, explains Dionysus's second birth from the thigh of his father Zeus and his subsequent release to worshippers in a stream of hallucinogenic urine. Yet Dionysus's source of intoxication has always been politely attributed by Greek scholars to wine, and Ambrosia is identified in the Oxford English Dictionary with asclepias (milk weed); and by various Encyclopedias with almost every sort of plant except mushrooms.

The Norse berserks were magicians and sages, and seem to have used the scarlet Amanita muscaria, as did the Korjaks, for inducing prophecies. They were called Berserks (Bear-shirts) because they worshipped the Bear goddess, which accounts for our Great Bear constellation, and wore bear skins in her honor. Their cult was suppressed in the eleventh century A.D. by Christian converts, not only in Scandinavia but in Iceland, where dwarf-birches in the center of the island provided the berserks with their amanita.

I have eaten the Mexican hallucinogenic mushroom psilocybe Heimsii in Gordon Wasson's company, with the intention of visiting the Mexican paradise called Tlalocan to which it gives access. The god Tlaloc, who was toadheaded, corresponded exactly with Agni and Dionysus. I also wanted to know whether I had been right in supposing that all religious paradises except the Christian (which is based on a first century Eastern potentate's court), such as the Hebrew, the Sumerian, the Indian, the Mexican, the Polynesian and the Greek (known as the Garden of Hesperides) were not only very much alike but corresponded also with the individual paradises seen by such mystics as the English poet Henry Vaughan, the Silurist. The word paradise means 'orchard' in the Semitic languages; an orchard-garden of fruit trees, flowers and running water. Yes, I had guessed right, though there are, I believe, certain dissimilarities: for instance, elephants appear in the Indian paradise and in others the inevitable serpent, familiar to readers of the Paradise chapter in Genesis, may appear as it did for me, as an intricately patterned gold chain. A bright snake-like formation is, by the way, a common symptom of a cerebral deoxygenization induced by hallucinogenic drugs; and seeing snakes is a common occurrence among alcoholics, saints who starve themselves, drowning sailors and sufferers from meningitis. My experiences included not only an orchard Paradise where one can see sound, hear colours, and watch trees growing leaf by leaf, but a paradise of jewels like that described in the Book of Ezekiel XXVIII, 13-14.

The psilocybe mushroom used in the Mexican rites is small, brown in color, slender-stalked and bitter; but sculptural evidence from Central America suggests that it had supplanted the Amanita muscaria in ritual use, probably because it was easier to obtain and because the hang-over did not last so long. The same change seems to have occurred in Greece: the discovery of a new hallucinogenic mushroom, a stropharia, or a panaeolus, which, unlike the Amanita muscaria, could be ground up and baked in sacrificial cakes for religious use in the Mysteries without losing its powers. When, according to the Greek myth, the Corn Goddess Demeter visited Eleusis, the Attic city where the Mysteries were to be celebrated for another two thousand years, she is said to have ordered Triptolemus, son of the local King, to drive around the civilized world in a chariot drawn by snakes, spreading the arts of agriculture as he went. This myth is clearly deceptive. Corn had been sown and harvested in Palestine for several thousands of years before Demeter's people arrived at Eleusis. What may have happened is that the local priestess sent a message about the newly discovered mushroom to priests and priestesses throughout the civilized world-hence the snakes in Triptolemus's chariot. This, if so, would explain why the nature and source of the original Soma has been forgotten in India for so many centuries. The supply from the birch groves of the High Himalayas seems to have been cut off by enemy action, and placebos, such as asclepias, substituted for it until eventually its place was taken in Brahman ritual, after the receipt of Triptolemus's message, by a better, more manageable and more accessible sacred mushroom.

In 1957 at my suggestion Mr. Wasson and the famous mycologist Dr. Roger Heim, Director of the Musee de l'Homme at Paris, visited the New Guinea Highlands from whence had come reports of a mushroom cult. They were able to attend. a Bird of Paradise courtship ceremony danced by Stone Age men and women under the influence of a sacred mushroom. The specimen that Wasson and Heim were offered proved, however, unhallucinogenic.

This may have meant either that the tribal elders deceived their visitors for religious reasons by giving them some ineffective substitute or that the tribe, having emigrated there from a place where a truly hallucinogenic mushroom grew, had been reduced to using this other variety as a placebo.

Another variety of the Amanita muscaria grows south of the fortieth parallel, with the pine as its host-tree, and is equally hallucinogenic. That it was ritually used in Biblical times is suggested by an unwritten Hebrew taboo on mushrooms, broken only by the non-orthodox. (Arabs, by the way, are mycophagous, which perhaps accounts for mushroom eating in those parts of Southern Europe occupied by the Saracens during the early Middle Ages.) I have elsewhere suggested that the golden 'ermrods' laid up in the Ark together with a pot of hallucinogenic manna really represented sacred mushrooms. A concealed reference to their use appears in the Book of Judges: the unlikely story of how Samson collected three hundred foxes and sent them into the Philistine's cornfields with torches tied to their tails. The Palestinian fox is not gregarious and the task of capturing three hundred of them, at the rate of one or two a day, and feeding them all until he had collected the full number would have been a senselessly exhausting one. Besides, how could he make sure that the foxes would run into the cornfields and keep the torches alight? The truth seems to be that Salnson organized a battalion of raiders-three hundred was the conventional Hebrew battalion strength, as appears in the story of Gideon-and sent them out with torches to burn the Philistines' corn. Indeed, in the 1948 Jewish War of Liberation a raiding battalion was named 'Samson's Foxes'. But why foxes? Because the juice of the Amanita muscaria mushrooms (which still grow under the pines of Mount Tabor) could be laced with ivy juice or wine to make the raiders completely fearless, and because this variety, when dried, is fox-coloured. So are other mushrooms, such as the popular chanterelle which the Russians call lisichka, 'little fox'; but to clarify its meaning the Bible specifies 'little foxes with fire in their tails'. In the Song of Solomon the Shunemite bride, about to take part in a sacred marriage, urges her lover to fetch her 'the little foxes that spoil the vines, for my vines have tender grapes'. She means that Solomon must fortify his manhood with mushroom-juice laced with wine, the better to enjoy her young beauty.

Why mycophobes called mushrooms 'toad's bread' or 'toadstools' can readily be explained. When the toad is attacked or scared the warts on its back exude bufonenin, the poison secreted in the white hallucinogenic warts of the Amanita muscaria. In ancient Greece the toad was the emblem of Argos, the leading state of the Peloponnese, the emblems of the two other states being also connected with the mushroom: namely fox and serpent. This division into states had been made by a legendary king named Phoroneus, which seems a form of Phryneus, meaning 'Toad-man'. The capital city was Mycenae ('Mushroom City') said to have been built by Phoroneus's successor Perseus ('the destroyer') who, according to Pausanicus, had found a mushroom growing on the site beside a spring of water. The toad was also the emblem of Tlalóc, the Mexican God of Inspiration, and appears surrounded by mushrooms in an Aztec mural painting of Tlalócan, his Paradise.

The Slavs are not mycophobic, probably because their remote ancestors were nomads on the treeless steppes and unacquainted with Amanita muscaria. Their fermented mare's milk, called kavasse, satisfied their need for occasional intoxication. Like the Arabs in their desert poverty they had learned to eat any growing plant or living animal that was not poisonous. Bavaria is mycophagous, while the rest of Germany is mycophobic, simply because it was once invaded by Slavs. " End of Graves

From Wikipedia:
In Russian tales, Baba Yaga is portrayed as a hag who flies through the air in a mortar, using the pestle as a rudder and sweeping away the tracks behind her with a broom made out of silver birch. She lives in a log cabin that moves around on a pair of dancing chicken legs, and/or surrounded by a palisade with a skull on each pole. The keyhole to her front door is a mouth filled with sharp teeth; the fence outside is made

with human bones with skulls on top, often with one pole lacking its skull, leaving space for the hero or heroes. In another legend, the house does not reveal the door until it is told a magical phrase: Turn your back to the forest, your front to me.

In some tales, the house is connected with three riders: one in white, riding a white horse with white harness, who is Day; a red rider, who is the Sun; and one in black, who is Night. Baba Yaga is served by invisible servants inside the house. She will explain the riders if asked, but may kill a visitor who inquires about the servants.

Baba Yaga is sometimes shown as an antagonist, and sometimes as a source of guidance; there are stories where she helps people with their quests, and stories in which she kidnaps children and threatens to eat them. Seeking out her aid is usually portrayed as a dangerous act. An emphasis is placed on the need for proper preparation and purity of spirit, as well as basic politeness.

Baba Yaga in Polish folklore differs in details. For example, the Polish Baba Jaga's house has only one chicken leg. Monstrous witches living in gingerbread houses are also commonly named Baba Jaga. Baba Jaga, flying on a mop, wearing black and red striped folk cloth of Swietokrzyskie Mountains is an unofficial symbol of Kielce region (it is connected with legendary witches sabbaths on Lysa Góra mountain).

The name differs within the various Slavic languages. It is spelled "Baba Jaga" in Czech and Slovak (though Czech and Slovak also use Ježibaba). In Slovene, the words are reversed, producing Jaga Baba. In Russian, Bulgarian and Ukrainian it is transliterated as Baba Yaga (or Baba Yaha in Ukrainian). In South Slavic languages and traditions, there is a similar old witch, written Baba Roga in Croatian and Bosnian, andin Serbian and Macedonian.

The name of Baba Yaga is composed of two elements. Baba means "grandmother" or "old woman" (Author's Note: Remember the priests of Kaaba to this day are still known as the 'Sons of the Old Woman.') in most Slavic languages. Yaga is probably a diminutive of the feminine name Jadwiga (with variant forms Jagusia/Jadzia, etc.). Jadwiga, in turn, is simply a Slavicized form of the Germanic Hedwig, and thus has no particular meaning in the Slavic languages. However, some etymologists have conjectured other origins for Yaga; for example, Vasmer mentions the Proto-Slavic eg..

In the folk tale Vasilissa the Beautiful, recorded by Alexander Afanasyev (Narodnye russkie skazki, vol 4, 1862), the young girl of the title is given three impossible tasks that she solves using a magic doll given to her by her mother.

In the Christianised version of the story, Vasilissa is sent to visit Baba Yaga on an errand and is enslaved by her, but the hag's servants — a cat, a dog, a gate, and a tree — help Vasilissa to escape because she has been kind to them. In the end, Baba Yaga is turned into a crow. (Author's Note: Remember who else turned into a crow?)

Chapter Nine: Nutrition and Exercise

"An organism supplied with a diet adequate to, or preferably in excess of, all mineral requirements may so utilize these elements as to produce immunity from infection quite beyond anything we are able to produce artificially by our present method of immunization..."

Senate Document #264, June 1936

Nutrition is incredibly important to our bodies which is why I would like to go over a few things I have picked-up along the way regarding it. About twenty years ago '60 Minutes' did a study on a small Japanese village whose population well exceeded an 80-year life-expectancy. The purpose of the study was to determine why its younger population of adults that adopted a western diet have all seemed to pass away while their parents lived on. '60 Minutes' concluded it was the high amount of hyaluronic acid present in their diet due to the fact that they grew potatoes surrounding the village in the hillsides instead of rice.

Hyaluronic Acid is also known as hyaluronan or hyaluronate or simply just as HA, is considered a carbohydrate. Chemically structured to be thousands of times longer than a regular carbohydrate molecule HA binds to water easily to become viscous in texture much like jelly. Hyaluronic acid is present in its largest amounts in your eyeballs and joints, however it is present throughout your entire body. It is produced in every cell, its primary function is to allow nutrients to flow to cells that do not come in contact with blood-vessels and to allow toxins to flow away from them as well, no less important is the job of lubricating our entire bodies all the way from our hearts, to our knees and everything below, above and in-between. It has been said more than once that HA may very well be the single most important compound in the structure of the human body.

One gentleman was even a smoker, he stated that no one has told him to quit nor has he ever had a reason to. This fact is in direct correlation with the statement provided by the Senate document at the top of this page. Any person who has adequate nutrition should produce enough HA to cleanse the body of unwanted toxins. Have you ever seen the commercials on TV where they are selling pads that you stick in your shoes that absorb toxins from the soles of your feet, usually marketed as ancient Eastern wisdom. Well this is because gravity causes the toxins to ooze down your legs into the pads of your feet and out the bottom. If you sit too often and watch TV or read too much you will allow those toxins to affect your precious organs around your midsection causing premature cancer to develop.

Nutrition is not just the only part of living a long life, exercise is a must as well. The lymphatic system is a set of hollow tubes that run through your body which have no way of propelling their contents except from the movement caused by your physical activity. I view them as a gutter for your body to send toxins to before they reach the brain. The HA present in your body allows your cells a vehicle to herd the toxins in on their way to the lymphatic system where the toxins travel down your legs and out the bottom of your feet which is why your feet itch and burn when you have too many toxins from the foods you consume. The Egyptians believed that all illnesses were caused by the foods they ate and they were right. They fasted for three days every month to allow their body extra time to detoxify itself just to make sure they didn't overload their bodies of toxins.

Somewhere around the number of twenty-four billion cells deteriorate in the body everyday, you require nutrients to constantly rebuild your plethora of deteriorating cells on a daily basis. You might be thinking you need to run out and buy some vitamins or you might be feeling assured that you have been giving yourself plenty of nutrients because you're already on a vitamin regimen. Synthetic vitamins are actually incredibly detrimental to your health.

When your body digests a food like a carrot, it utilizes all of the nutrients in the stomach to aid in digestion, however when your body tries to digest synthetic vitamins like those added in many foods and advertised as good for you, you body cannot. This is due to the fact that your stomach is lacking the necessary co-factors required to break-down the vitamin, co-factors like enzymes and other vitamins. Now because your body cannot digest the contents in your stomach your body immediately searches its tissue, bone, muscle, and internal organs for these necessary and vital nutrients just in order to be able to digest what is in your stomach. That means you are actually stripping your entire body of vital nutrients when you think you are giving yourself nutrients.

Too much Vitamin C is bad for you, but without it your cells will literally fall apart and you will begin to bleed out of your orifices. I see many companies advertising vitamins that they have added into the ingredients like B2, C, and others. When you have large amounts of synthetic vitamin C in your stomach you are constantly stripping your body of enzymes and nutrients necessary for proper function and health just to be able to digest the synthetic vitamin C. Then any vitamin C that you do receive is not anywhere near enough to repair the damage you have caused putting it into your body. Synthetic vitamins have been linked to a whole slew of health problems including synthetic vitamin E and beta carotene causing lung cancer and heart attack, synthetic vitamin C causing hardened arteries in men, synthetic vitamin A causing birth-defects and various synthetics are causing liver damage.

The human body was designed to move, we evolved into the creatures that we did specifically because of our ability to evade predators and survive. We didn't evade predators by lying dormant and hiding; we ran. We were continuously running and we were very warm, which allowed the fluids in our bodies to move easily carrying the toxins away from our important internal organs and our most importantly our brains. I think of toxins like a clothing iron, if they are constantly moving they do no harm, but if you are stagnate then they start to cause damage.

I must admit that for years I was falsely under the impression that Psilocybin mushrooms were responsible for our brains expanding during our evolution. I felt that it was more likely than the other argument for brain expansion at the time which was eating meat. I recently found a paper ascribing heat exhaustion and our endurance running abilities which allowed those evolving who survived predation to give birth to children with slightly more brain cells each generation to allow the brain stem insulation from outside heat and to take over brain functions when the brain cells do die. The brain is designed in a way that allows the brain areas to overlap their functionality. Meaning multiple areas of the brain can perform multiple functions and even learn functions they never knew before or were not required to know.

I am under the belief now that our brains expanded due to the fact that our bodies recognized the benefit of having additional brain cells and therefore produced offspring with more which allowed our ancestors to perform some creative thinking skills, that after practicing and development were capable of creating our civilization today. Without the will to survive and the struggle to get here we would have never existed at all. It is as if nature was designed in a way as to create consciousness from our struggle but I'm not saying it was. One thing is for sure though, recent studies have proven that whenever population was dense cranial capacity began to diminish and whenever population was sparse cranial capacity would begin to enlarge; there is obviously a direct link between fighting to survive, and brain expansion.

A good friend of mine mentioned carrot juice as being really important for my health, so I decided to do some research and here is just some of what I discovered. A ten-year study coming out of the Netherlands regarding carrot intake in relation to cardiovascular disease found that out of the four color groups focused on, green, red/purple, orange/yellow, and white, the deepest shades of orange came out on top as most protective against CVD.

Roughly twelve-thousand years ago the ice-age started to recede allowing grasses to spring forth. We probably noticed other creatures eating a lot of wheat and decided to copy them. This ancient wheat species was called Einkorn and contains only fourteen chromosomes. A few thousand years later somehow another type of wild grass cross-pollinated with the ancient wheat creating a new form of wheat with twenty-eight chromosomes, this wheat is called Emmer wheat. Around the middle-ages this Emmer wheat again cross-pollinated with another wild grass creating Spelt which contains a whopping forty-two chromosomes.

Now this may seem a bit out of left field but there is an ancient tribe of people who are not very well-known today called the Yezidi. They have long held a rivalry with Muslims and are currently being persecuted in large numbers and are considered devil-worshippers. However the Yezidi have no devil in their religion.

Tony Lagourani's comments on a Yazidi prisoner in his book Fear Up Harsh: An Army Interrogator's Dark Journey through Iraq, "There's a lot of mystery surrounding the Yazidi, and a lot of contradictory information. But I was drawn to this aspect of their beliefs: Yazidi don't have a Satan. Malak Ta'us, an archangel, God's favorite, was not thrown out of heaven the way Satan was. Instead, he descended, saw the suffering and pain of the world, and cried. His tears, thousands of years' worth, fell on the fires of hell, extinguishing them. If there is evil in the world, it does not come from a fallen angel or from the fires of hell. The evil in this world is man-made. Nevertheless, humans can, like Malak Ta'us, live in this world but still be good."

Why do I bring this up you wonder? Because the Yezidi claim to be the oldest religion on the face of the Earth and have what they claim to be the original Holy Bible that they call the "Black Book". From the 'Black Book', "He created Adam and put in him a soul, out of His own might. Then He commanded Jibrâ´îl to put Adam in paradise, and ordered that he might eat from all the fruits of paradise. But He commanded that he should not eat wheat. A hundred years later Tâwûs Malâk said to God, "What is this? Adam and his offspring are going to be numerous." God said to him, "Into your hands I have given this matter to minister." Then he came to Adam and said, "Have you eaten wheat?" He said, "No, because God forbade me." He said to him, "Eat of it. Things will prove better than they are now." So he ate, and after he did eat Tâwûs Malâk caused his belly to become swollen. He put him out of paradise, left him alone, and went up to heaven. Adam suffered a great deal from the pain in his belly, for he had no outlet. Then God sent a bird which came and pecked an opening for him. Adam was relieved. Jibrâ´îl absented himself from him one hundred years, during which he became sorrowful and wept."

So let us recapitulate what we have read now, after the ice started melting and allowing grasses to grow forth from the ground, our oldest ancestors got the bright idea to eat wheat to alleviate their hunger. Initially it did cause problems which indicated to the Yezidi that is was not healthy for us to eat, however hunger and starvation prevailed and our ability to solve unique problems allowed us to develop ways of processing the wheat that would allow us to digest it more easily. That does not mean that it is good for us or that we should not stop eating it immediately after an emergency ordeal like the depletion of our food supply caused from woolly rhinoceros, mammoth, cave bear, cave lion, saber-toothed cats, and dire wolves dying off due to heat exhaustion.

There are many things to consider, I find more and more everyday that the single fear which encroaches my soul day-in and day-out is that when I decide to publish this book I'll start learning more than ever. The challenge of living with Fukushima is proving to be a formidable adversary. Especially when you take into account the immense lifestyle pattern change necessary. I don't want to lie to anyone, the truth of the matter is that you cannot live with Fukushima.

At least the old you can't, the sugar-filled, candida-incubating, last-drop-of-soy-licking version of you will die in a timely manner whether you want to or not. Your only chance at a life-on-the-west-coast is going to be had by a rebirth.

Now I can't tell you everything I know, partly because I would feel bad and partly because I don't have that kind of willpower to devote that much time into this book, I will definitely write later but for now I have priorities and no money, I'm still changing my habits, I have found this is easier done when going slow like changing gears in a vehicle with a manual transmission, try hopping into a six-speed-gearbox-equipped car and hammer the gas and shift the gears. Your car is slow, trust me, hence you think shifting is easy, it's all relative. The first time I drove a real fast car I realized I couldn't drive at all, let alone shift gears.

The first thing you need to do is get some rest. Sleep is the single most important thing a person needs. Exercise is just as important as sleep, can you comprehend what I just said fully and completely. You were with me on the sleep part but I lost you on the exercise notion. Just as important means if you are sleeping eight hours a day you should be at an agitated heart-rate for at least eight hours a day minimum.

All life is energy; everything living has some energy in it. Food is a source of energy. All energy comes from the Sun; everything living has some Sunlight in it. Sunlight is our main source of energy. Plants are a second-generation source of energy. Meat is third-generation sunlight. I look at seeds/nuts/berries like gasoline for a combustion engine and meat/seafood like the oil. The oil is very necessary but it is not a source of energy.

I eat mainly high moisture/high fiber fruits and veggies and I drink water. What a concept, how primitive. Yet, how lively as well eh? The less you eat, the longer you live. Period. The more infrequently you eat the longer you live. Period. The more-often you have insulin in your blood stream the less you produce HGH(human growth hormone) and the more you produce the aging hormones that cause cells to die-off and regenerate. The thing is, you can only die-off and regenerate so much until you finally... die.

The less you eat the more HGH is being produced. If you eat once a day, a really decent meal, you will live to be one-hundred-years-old I guarantee it! This constant eating of three meals a day and two in-between is killing us. Not to mention the food pyramid is upside and backwards! You aren't a cow, you aren't supposed to eat grains! Oat are unique in that they are soft on our intestines. Wheat is like glass, especially whole wheat and is the number one cause of irritable bowel syndrome, stomach ulcers, intestinal cancer, and a whole slew of other ailments. Wheat shreds the little hairs off your intestinal walls that help digest your food, then when they are gone it shreds your intestines and bleed out the rectum and wonder why and blame it on stress!

Everything in moderation my friend. Even too much whole grain wheat is bad for you. Shredded wheat and milk from cows that eat grass for breakfast, two slices of whole wheat toast with tuna and pickles for lunch, maybe some whole-wheat pasta with light vinaigrette dressing for dinner. The average American woman is probably eating too much grain. Then when your body tries to expel all the toxins in its system, whether it is yeast or something else, you are told to ingest a chemical composition that will inhibit your body's ability to detoxify itself by letting its mucus membranes drain.

Essentially western medicine has shown itself to be geared more towards causing you to die slowly by letting you rot from the inside-out and it is okay as long as you look good on the outside. The United States of America is now having discussion regarding taxing fat consumption. As if fat is a bad thing, they should be taxing sugar consumption, they would make a lot more money off of that anyways. Not only that but anytime the general population catches wind of something remotely unhealthy for them they are provided with an even unhealthier alternative under the guise of it being more healthy.

For instance, there is no gluten-free product that doesn't supplant wheat with anything else but white starches that up your blood-sugar levels more than cotton candy. Sugar-free drinks are chalk full of brain-tumor causing artificial sweeteners. Which brings me to chalk, speaking of chalk, did you know one-half of a percent of your salt is simply chalk dust used to make sure the salt granules come out of the shaker faster so you buy more salt?

Table salt is a mineral, rocks are made up of minerals. We aren't designed to digest rocks, not salt, and not chalk, it destroys your internal organs, research chalk dust in our food and research salt. Chalk dust can and will end up wherever it happens to find itself lodged in your body, literally, if your body doesn't have enough magnesium to absorb the calcium into your bones it will calcify your entire being, every internal organ and every cell, turn you into one big bone-headed moron.

Magnesium protects the mitochondria which is the powerhouse of the cell from free radical damage. The higher the magnesium levels

in a cell the healthier it is. It should also have low calcium levels. If
there is an excess of calcium in out diet then there becomes an excess of
calcium in our blood being supplied to every cell in our entire body. If
there is too much calcium the mitochondria calcifies and this is the
beginning of the aging process. After the mitochondria calcify, slowly
but surely so do all of the internal organs.

Too much calcium negates the anti-oxidant effects of vitamin D
altogether and magnesium is necessary for the absorption of vitamin D
at all. Vitamin D lowers insulin resistance. Scientist now know that
insulin resistance can and will occur is all organs and leading
researchers now believe that Alzheimer's disease is simply insulin
resistance of the brain. The thyroid gland regulates levels of calcium in
your body by secreting a hormone after processing vitamin D and I just
told you how important low calcium levels in every cell of your body
were.

I have heard from many women, typically the small frail type
one would suspect of coming down with osteoporosis from lack of
proper nutrition due to dieting and too much low-fat non-dairy
products, that they suffered horrible side-effects due to doctors
pressuring them to take large amounts of calcium supplements. These
supplements obviously caused a huge abundance of calcium in their
cells and build-up and calcification of their joints and internal organs
started to occur at the same time as did their bones begin to weaken.

Cow's milk is not good for you for multiple reasons. It has an
extremely high calcium ratio. Remember that you need lots of
magnesium to build strong bones, not calcium. More likely than not you
will always have enough calcium, not magnesium. How is your

mitochondria supposed to create adequate amounts of hyaluronic acid if it is calcified? Remember hyaluronic acid is created by every cell in your entire body and is responsible for bringing oxygen and nutrients to the far reaches of your flesh that your blood vessels aren't touching.

Let's discuss fat, fat is not a bad thing... at all actually. If you eat too much fat instead of storing it your body will expel it in the form of diarrhea. This is because fat contains a lot of oils and amino acids and your body doesn't need them and so it expels them. Eating fat doesn't make you store fat, eating fat causes you to burn calories faster thus upping your metabolism. If I eat sugar instead of fat my body receives empty calories meaning I receive tons of energy that my body must do something with, my metabolism slows down almost to a halt entirely and I go into a diabetic coma.

Sugar contains absolutely no vitamins or nutrients that your body needs, not only to digest the sugar itself, but to go on living. So what happens when you ingest sugar that provides you energy in massive amounts that you can't do anything with? Tumors. That's right, even though your body can't use the sugar for anything other than temporary immediate energy cells that are becoming tumors actually feed off of the sugar in your blood stream.

Not just tumors, but biological organisms living in your body thrive off of sugar as well(actually better). Not only does sugar decrease your immune system's ability to function by over fifty percent while it's in your bloodstream due to its viscosity but while it is inhibiting the flow of traffic allowing your body's defenses to come to the rescue it is propelling every single alien cell in your body. It's as if sugar is a giant shield for disease with a little water bottle attached behind it that the enemy can nourish itself with some sort of rocket-fuel and I'd say sugar is between one-third and one-half of your average American's diet today literally.

I know of two studies involving rats that you will find alarming to say the least. The first involves rats that have been fed the common probiotic lactobacillus and their counterparts who have not. When a healthy normal rat is dropped into a bowl of warm water they struggle for a few minutes and give up. This reaction is due to the extreme adrenaline rush the rat experiences due to the intensity of the situation obviously. Rats who have been fed the probiotic lactobacillus however keep continuing to struggle. Not until the person running the experiment would retrieve the rat would its vitals return to normal.

The scientists running the research project speculated that the lactobacillus may be altering the brain via signals sent from the large nerve coming from the rats guts. So they clipped it. And sure enough, the rats returned to normal, struggling for a few minutes and stopping only to float on the water in despair. They figured out that the bacteria lactobacillus would send extra serotonin from the stomach to the brain via this nerve causing the rats to freak out but only freak out say one-third as much as if their system was full of just adrenaline. I believe the bacteria discovered it was under less assault from our bodies defenses when we weren't so full of adrenaline and simply for its living room comfort it chooses to mitigate the temperature of its environment per-say like you would in the shower by adjusting the hot and cold levers.

The second study involves rats that have been fed the equivalent to a western diet. Healthy rats were dropped into a bowl of water with a pedestal in the center and observed to witness how long they took to reach safety or climb onto the pedestal provided and take a rest from the terrifying swim. It took them on average five and one-half seconds to reach the pedestal.

The other rats, the ones that were fed the equivalent to a two-thousand calorie-a-day diet consisting of our modern food pyramid... fifty-five seconds. The female scientist conducting the study was in the process of blow-drying one of the test subjects who she stated, "the rats have essentially become demented animals who cannot remember what they learned after even just a day."

Products labels as wheat flour actually contain what is known as refined white flour; whole wheat flour is actually wheat flour. Since the 1920s the US Food and Drug Administration required refined white flour to be enriched with iron and other vitamins since any animals that were fed refined white flour died but only after developing severe neurological diseases.

Enrichment means loading the refined white flour with iron after it has been bleached. The iron used is not the same iron that you would receive eating foods that contained iron. And there is a lot of it, no balance whatsoever as would be found in nature. Remember what I mentioned earlier in regards to what would happen if you ingested too much of one thing and no co-factors?

Iron poisoning is very real, iron takes the place of over one-thousand enzyme receptors which leads to all sorts of neurological diseases. It is essential in oxygen transfer and while not enough iron can be bad too much can be fatal as well, not to mention if you like orange juice. Vitamin C causes the body to absorb as much iron as it can. When you become full of iron instead of other things you need an excess amount of oxygen is attracted to your cells due to the relationship between iron and oxygen.

When this happens it is called oxidant damage or free radical damage, a major cause of inflammation. The isolated oxygen molecules destroy body tissue. H2O2, hydrogen peroxide, water- with an extra oxygen molecule. You use it to kill bacteria when you get a scrape on your arm because nothing can live in the presence of pure oxygen. We are gassing our cells with oxygen that is supposed to go elsewhere and it is lethal. Iron oxide occurs when several atoms of oxygen join together with iron.

Because iron transfers oxygen it supplies other bacteria with growth that thrive on smaller amounts of oxygen. This is one of the main causes of chronic infections in our population. An imbalance in our bodies of iron will lead to cancer. In medical literature diabetes is known as bronze diabetes, but most researchers today believe that iron toxicity is more-to-blame.

Don't think you are off the hook yet fish, Parkinson's, Alzheimer's, violence, ADHD, autism all have direct links well-documented regarding iron overload. Iron accumulates in our liver and the Chinese used to call it the seat of iron, however it also loves to store itself it the anger centers of the brain and thus you see the angry meat-eater with dementia being visited by his happy children who get to see their father being fed with such dignity and class at such an institution.

Manganese also plays a pivotal role in many physiological processes. Studies have shown that high levels of manganese ingested through drinking water led to significantly lower test scores of intellectual function, hyperactivity, and behavioral disorders in children.

Manganese and iron share the same pathways and thus iron toxicity can lead to manganese deficiency and vice-versa.

From the World Health Organizations' "Background document for development of WHO Guidelines for Drinking-water Quality" titled, "Manganese in Drinking-water" and can be found at http://www.who.int/water_sanitation_health/dwq/chemicals/manganese.pdf -

"This study also reported that the average manganese level in hair in children exhibiting learning disabilities was significantly increased (0.434 ?g/g) compared with that in children who exhibited normal learning ability (0.268 ?g/g)... Manganese is present in all tissues of the body, the highest levels usually being found in the liver, kidney, pancreas and adrenals (Tipton & Cook, 1963; Sumino et al., 1975). It accumulates preferentially in certain regions of the brain in infants and young animals (Zlotkin & Buchanan, 1986; Kontur & Fechter, 1988)... The central nervous system is the chief target of manganese toxicity... Neurotoxicity is a known effect of long-term exposure to inhaled manganese in humans and animals, but the potential for neurotoxicity resulting from oral exposure is less well characterized. Muscular weakness and lower limb rigidity were observed in four male rhesus monkeys given oral doses... 4.4 Reproductive and developmental toxicity: The results of several studies in rats and mice indicate that the ingestion of manganese can delay reproductive maturation in male animals (ATSDR, 2000)... An epidemiological study in Japan described adverse effects in humans consuming manganese dissolved in drinking-water, probably at a concentration close to 28 mg/l (Kawamura et al., 1941). The manganese was derived from 400 dry-cell batteries buried near a drinking-water well. Fifteen cases of poisoning were reported among 25 persons examined, with symptoms including lethargy, increased muscle tone, tremor and mental disturbances. The most severe effects were seen in elderly people; less severe effects were seen in younger people, and effects were absent in children aged 1–6 years. However, the level of exposure to manganese was poorly quantified, and the people were also exposed to high levels of zinc. The rapid onset and progression of the symptoms and the recovery of some patients prior to mitigation of the manganese-contaminated well water suggest that exposure to other chemicals may also have been a factor in the presentation of symptoms. An epidemiological study was conducted in Greece to investigate the possible correlation between long-term (i.e. more than 10 years) manganese exposure from water and neurological effects in elderly people (Kondakis et al., 1989). The levels of manganese in the drinking-water of three different geographical areas were 3.6–14.6 ?g/l in the control area and 81–253 ?g/l and 1800–2300 ?g/l in the test areas. The authors concluded that progressive increases in the manganese concentration in drinking-water are associated with a progressively higher prevalence of neurological signs of chronic manganese poisoning and higher manganese concentrations in the hair of older persons."

Dentist mention that vegetarians have the absolutely worst teeth out of any patients they ever treat due to the high amount of fruit they consume. Wheat is not meant to be eaten, remember this, it destroys your intestines, makes you hungry at the same time it reduces how many nutrients you can absorb. Sugar feeds everything in your body except your body. You need certain ratios of certain ingredients in your body, like potassium/sodium balance, omega-6/omega3 balance. You cannot put salt on your meat people. You cannot put salt on anything period actually. It might be a nice game to play to dull the intensity of certain fun foods, but not as a staple in the human diet. Remember that calcium doesn't build strong bones, you need a healthy phosphorus/calcium ratio and milk has an unhealthy ratio. Calcium will calcify every cell in your body, you need magnesium to allow manganese to penetrate and harden your bones, not calcium. Be aware of heavy metals that are depressants like manganese and iron toxicity in your well-water, you need manganese but not in large quantities in your drinking water.

Epilogue

The first instance I felt more compelled to study the history of the use of the Amanita muscaria than any other subject is when I stumbled upon it depicted in a "Today's Featured Picture" article on Wikipedia of Baba Yaga. That was seven years ago, seven years before that I started studying religion and spirituality. This book is fourteen years in-the-making, I hope you found it worth the read.

Thank-You Sincerely,
Michael Jerry Mitchell

We cannot fail to recognize 'the Lady of the Labyrinth'

Da-pu-ri-to-jo Po-ti-ni-ja

Bibliography

Ardrey, Robert, African Genesis. New York, 1961.

Biale, David, The Goddess and the Bull. 2007.

Carl, Jung, Alchemical Studies.

Collins, Andrew, Tutankhamun The Exodus Conspiracy. New York, 2003.

Guthrie, W.K.C, The Greeks and Their Gods. New York, 1950.

Heinrich, Clark, Magic Mushrooms in Religion and Alchemy. 2002.

Herodotus, The Histories. 440 BCE.

Leakey, Richard, Origins Reconsidered. 1992.

Link, Mark J, These Stones Will Shout. New York, 1975.

McDonald, William A, Progress Into the Past. New York, 1967.

McKenna, Terrence, The Sacred Mushroom Seeker. 1990.

Nilsson, Martin P, The Mycenaean Origin of Greek Mythology. Cali: L.A., 1932.

Plutarch, Nine Greek Lives: The Rise and Fall of Athens.

Robert, Graves, The Greek Myths. New York, 1955.

Russell, Dan, Shamanism and the Drug Propaganda. 1998.

Wiesehofer, Josef , Ancient Persia. 2000

Xenophon, Anabasis

Index

aaron 58, 63, 74, 78, 112
abraham 65, 76
abu'l 91
acacia-wood 96
achaeans 43, 47
acrisius 96
acropolis 19
adam 9, 35, 36, 49, 83, 89, 104,
105, 140, 165, 166
adamas 83
adamic 37
adom 33, 34, 37, 48, 49, 104
adon 36, 54, 75
adonai 54, 76
adoni 29
adoniad 54
adoniads 54, 55
adonis 14, 29, 36, 37, 54, 55, 56
adrenaline 172
adrenals 175
adrop 9
adyton 23
aegean 59
aegidius 8
aeolian 78
aeolians 43
aether 86
aetheric 93
aethra 18
afanasyev 159
african 50, 62, 180
africanus 105
agamedes 21, 24
agaric 64, 81, 82, 114, 121, 122,
123, 124, 125, 126, 127, 128, 129,
130, 131, 150
agathon 20

agathos 23
agenor's 42
agni 151, 152, 153
aischylos 70
akhenaten 59, 60, 61, 62, 64
akhenaten's 60, 61, 64
akhenaton 58, 59, 62, 63, 64, 65, 67
akhenaton's 63, 67
akhetaten 60, 62
akkadian 41, 57, 74, 78
akkadian-babylonian 85
al-thill 78
al-uzza 78
alchemical 4, 8, 11, 12, 13, 14, 16,
71, 72, 87, 89, 91, 92, 94, 96, 121,
180
alchemist 4, 7, 8, 9, 71, 91
alchemists 16, 85, 86, 90, 92, 95, 97
alchemy 8, 13, 16, 17, 42, 50, 70,
82, 83, 90, 92, 94, 180
algeria 50
alzheimer's 170, 174
amaltheia's 80
amanita 5, 9, 16, 29, 32, 35, 37, 50,
68, 71, 74, 87, 88, 90, 94, 95, 99,
103, 104, 117, 118, 120, 125, 127,
131, 132, 140, 143, 150, 151, 153,
154, 155, 156, 157, 178
amarna 59, 60, 62, 85
ambrosia 120, 142, 143, 144, 150,
151, 152
amenhotep 60, 61, 62, 65, 66
ammenon 38
amnael 86, 87
amphibios 39
amrita 120
amun 60, 61, 62

amun-re 60
anedot 38
anedoti 38
anedots 38
angel 74, 75, 86, 87, 96, 125, 126, 127, 165
angels 86, 105, 106, 107, 110
anima 13, 84, 97
ankh 49, 61
ankhesenamun 61, 62
ankhesenpaaten 61
ankhsenpaaten 67
anoint 21, 141
anointed 10, 25, 71, 72, 77, 86
anointing 77
antas 51
ante-nicene 105
antediluvian 38
anthropomorphic 40
anthropos 7
antilegomena 95
aphrodisiac 147
aphrodite 30, 40, 44, 54, 55, 57
apocryphal 74
apollo 6, 18, 27, 59, 88
apollodorus 68
apollon 20, 24
apollonius 23, 69
apologies 115
apolytrosis 72
apostate 35
apotheosis 72
aqaba 62
aqua 86, 93, 95, 121
aquarium 13
aquinas 8, 90
arab 78
arabia 29, 75
arabian 40, 91
arabic 4, 76, 91

arabs 5, 65, 155, 157
aramaic 41, 55
araqiel 110
arcadia 78
arcana 90, 95
arcane 4, 5, 87, 89, 91, 92, 94
arcanum 93, 96, 98
archangel 101, 165
archbishop 72, 74, 81
archimedes 69, 70
ardrey 180
argive 79, 96
argives 42
argos 80, 97, 144, 157
arislei 12
aristarchus 69, 70
aristophanes 20, 23
aristotle 70
ark 77, 96, 120, 155
armaros 110
arnaldus 13
arsaces 40
artarus 45
artemis 27
arteries 163
arthur 59, 78, 82
artifex 8
aryan 45, 47
asclepias 153, 155
asclepius 56
ash-tree 80
asherah 113
ashington 115
ashtaroth 112
ashurnasirpal 52, 85
asia 29, 53, 59, 152
asiatic 62
assyrian 31, 39, 40, 52, 59
assyrians 40, 58
astarte 29, 43, 55, 78, 113

asteria 55
asterius 19
astral 55, 122
atabyrius 45
atargatis 78
athanasius 74
athena 19, 44, 45, 72
athenagoras 105
aton 64, 66, 67
attica 17, 19
attis 91
augeias's 43
augury 127
augustine 105
aulus 9
aurelia 14
aurelian 70
aurelii 71
aurora 8, 90
autism 174
aye 60, 61, 65
azazel 74, 77, 78, 110
baal 47, 54, 55, 56
baalath 57
baalim 112
baals 56
baba 157, 158, 159, 178
babylon 31, 36, 42, 78
babylonian 35, 36, 58, 85, 113
babylonians 33, 38, 58
bacchus 9, 10, 27, 28, 30, 35, 151
bacteria 172, 174
bactria 29
bahram 76
baitulos 11
balawat 52
balearic 51
balearics 148
balkans 148
balsam 141

baptism 141
baraqijal 110
barbarians 30
barbeliots 83
barley 25
barley-cakes 22
basilides 99, 141
basran 76, 77
bear 10, 36, 130, 131, 153, 166
bee 43, 79
bee-goddess 114
beehive 79
beer 151
bees 24, 30, 79, 80, 114
befana 116
belili 113
bennett 41, 114, 119
berosus 36, 38
berserk 131
berserker 131
berserks 143, 153
berthelot 97
bhang 29
birch 122, 150, 152, 155, 157
birch-groves 152
bird 44, 97, 155, 166
bird-faced 45
birds 6, 107, 113, 146
birth 12, 31, 58, 83, 89, 129, 139,
151, 152, 163
bishop 65, 72, 105
bishops 37, 39, 116, 117, 140
black 5, 42, 43, 71, 91, 125, 126,
128, 129, 158, 165
blacksmith 19
blitzen 121
blood-sugar 169
bo-opis 45
bodhi 83
boiotia 24

bond-maiden 65
boreas 114
bosnian 159
bovine 40
boy 9, 36, 43, 65, 103, 125, 126
boy-king 61
boy-surrogate 37
brahman 155
brain 161, 163, 164, 170, 172, 174, 175
branch 10, 36
branches 5, 6, 83, 89, 91, 96, 131
bread 12, 120, 156
bread-oven 21
britain 83, 115, 116
british 150
broad-face 42
bronze 21, 34, 40, 46, 47, 52, 174
buccinae 11
buddha 83, 134, 141
buddhism 141
buddhist 38, 120, 141
bufonenin 156
bulgarian 159
bull 19, 41, 43, 45, 47, 59, 68, 97, 180
bull-calf 78
bull-headed 19
bull-king 43
bulls 20, 41, 43
bunny 119
butcher 82
cabalistic 90
cactus 139
cadmus 88
caesarius 94
caffeine 139
cain 105
cairn 46
calcification 170

calcify 169, 170, 177
calcium 169, 170, 177
callimachus 69, 80
campestris 148
canaan 50
canaanites 50
canada 116
cancer 161, 163, 168, 174
candida-incubating 167
cannabis 29, 67, 99, 103, 104, 139
cannibalism 107
cannibalistic 107
canonical 80
cantankerous 146
carbuncle 15
cardinals 37, 117
carotene 163
carrot 162, 164
carthage 50, 55, 56
cassiodorus 91
cat 159
catholic 3, 31, 35, 37, 98, 105
cattle 42, 107
cecyon 144
cedar 52
celestial 97, 98, 122, 127, 131
celtic 23
celts 46
centaur 143
centaurs 30, 142, 143, 144, 146, 147
chaldaen 142
chaldea 33, 38
chaldean 35, 36, 38, 76
chaldeans 34, 38, 58
chaldee 9, 36
chalk 129, 169
chanterelle 156
chaos 16, 93
chapel 71

chariot 37, 49, 124, 154
charioteer 20
chariots 49, 50
chattels 80
chemica 97
chemmis 97
cherubim 71
chiddingstone 66
chief 48, 61, 62, 74, 78, 175
chief-priestess 19
chitin 109
christ 4, 12, 13, 27, 31, 59, 86, 91, 93, 95, 96, 98, 119, 126
christianity 63, 67, 73, 81, 84, 132
christmas 114, 115, 116, 117, 121, 122, 123, 124, 126, 127, 128, 130, 131, 132
chromosomes 164, 165
church 37, 72, 73, 81, 83, 98, 99, 106, 117, 119, 128
citadel 79
claudius 147, 150
cloven 81
clover 31, 120
cnossus 44
co-factors 162, 173
coal 90
cocaine 139
collyrium 94
colonialism 139
coma 171
commodianus 105
copernicus 70
corinth 147
corn 37, 154, 156
counter-sun 95
cow 42, 43, 44, 80, 168
cow-eyed 44
cow-us 41
cows 40, 44, 168

crabs 149
cranes 146
crateia 43
cretan 19, 43, 78, 80
crete 19, 43, 44, 46, 78
croatian 159
crone 42, 46, 80
cronus 113
cross 11, 31, 33, 34, 35, 82, 96
crown 19, 83
crowned 57, 83
crucified 13, 95
ctesias's 43
ctesibius 69, 70
cuchulain 45
cuckoo 79, 80
cult 34, 40, 46, 51, 55, 56, 63, 65, 67, 68, 79, 81, 153, 155
cults 29, 40, 59, 123
cuneiform 41, 50
custom 46, 114, 116, 130, 144
customs 24, 54
cybele 40
cyclopes 97
cyllene 46
cypress 52
cypriots 54
cyprus 55, 56
cyrene 72
cyril 72, 81
czech 158
d'ion-nusa 36
da-pu-ri-to-jo 179
dagon 38
daidalos 21, 25
daimon 20, 23, 26
daimonos 20
dam 37
damascus 55
danaans 97

danae 96, 97
dark 15, 81, 91, 95, 99, 125, 126, 127, 133, 165
darkness 26, 77
dasher 122
daustricus 12
delphi 6, 10, 24, 88
demi-god 59
demiurge 80, 114
democritus 85
demon 74, 77, 97
deoxygenization 154
devil 77, 97, 132, 133, 165
devil-worshippers 165
devils 97
devotees 48
devoured 9, 43
dew 19, 94
deya 145
diabetes 174
diodorus 53, 68, 80
dionysiac 30
dionysian 68
dionysic 107
dionysos 27, 31
dionysus 27, 29, 30, 34, 35, 40, 59, 68, 79, 132, 142, 143, 144, 151, 152, 153
dionysus's 143, 151, 152
distillatio 16, 90
distillation 16, 90
divination 34
divine 38, 43, 56, 85, 86, 87, 92, 95, 96, 99, 108, 109, 112, 121, 132, 142, 144
dodonan 45
dog 103, 159
double-axe 48, 68, 80
dragon 12, 14, 15, 38, 68, 90, 94, 98, 107

dragons 14, 38
dream 17, 60, 125, 126
duality 133
dung-mushroom 143
duplex 13
dwarf-birches 153
eagle 6, 83
earth-god 30
earth-goddess 46, 80
east 6, 29, 36, 37, 49, 78
easter 29, 37, 73, 76, 83, 118, 119, 120
eastern 46, 65, 153, 161
eaten 43, 78, 114, 122, 124, 144, 153, 165, 176
eben 9
eben-ezer 9
ebn-hat-tul 9
ecstasy 123, 131, 132, 143
edfu 87
edom 33, 62, 74, 77
edomite 41
edomites 40, 41, 74
eesha 49
egypt 27, 31, 33, 51, 52, 53, 59, 60, 61, 62, 66, 69, 73
egyptian 27, 35, 40, 49, 51, 52, 53, 54, 57, 58, 59, 62, 63, 66, 70, 73, 74, 75, 92, 112
el-bar 36
elf 115, 116
elias 16
elixir 71
en-zu 42
endor 109
energy 143, 167, 171
english 48, 76, 115, 116, 148, 153
enlightened 42
enlightenment 126
entheogen 35, 85

entheogenic 72, 73, 83, 85, 122, 123, 129, 132, 139, 140
entheogens 73, 123, 139
eros 13, 123
erythraean 38
eryx 79
esarhaddon 55
esau 33, 74
eshmun 55, 56
essene 99, 101
eternal 9, 31, 32, 36, 73, 96, 132
eternity 38, 126, 131, 132
ethiopia 27
ethnomycology 127, 148
euclid 69, 70
euphrates 47, 51, 59
euripides 20, 29, 70
europe 11, 42, 43, 46, 114, 129, 148, 149, 155
evil 14, 50, 82, 107, 165
ewaldus 8
excavations 50, 51
excavators 30
exile 81
exodus 36, 41, 62, 75, 180
expel 168, 171
eyes 3, 14, 37, 44, 71, 86, 94, 120, 152
ezekiel 154
ezeqeel 110
fairy 128
faith 11, 35, 62, 96, 140
fertility 29, 30, 85, 119, 139
festivals 76, 139
festivities 55
fingernail 90
fir 122
fire 5, 14, 15, 16, 68, 71, 75, 82, 86, 87, 90, 91, 92, 97, 98, 101, 112, 114, 118, 121, 128, 140, 151, 156

fire-wheel 45, 97
firmament 85, 86, 94
fish 38, 39, 43, 86, 91, 94, 174
fish-spear 48
flavius 105
flaying 89
fleece 72, 120
flesh 36, 59, 73, 95, 96, 104, 107, 108, 119, 120, 140, 171
floating 71
flower 139
flowers 91, 153
fly 6, 64, 81, 82, 118, 121, 122, 123, 124, 125, 126, 127, 128, 129, 130, 131, 146, 150
fly-amanite 147
flyagaric 29
food 7, 37, 52, 96, 120, 139, 142, 144, 146, 147, 149, 150, 151, 162, 166, 167, 168, 169, 173
foods 144, 161, 162, 173, 177
footprint 134
forest 158
forests 150, 157
fox-coloured 156
fox-lady 123
fresco 47, 71, 144
fruit 9, 12, 32, 68, 71, 72, 85, 91, 113, 120, 140, 153, 176
fruit-bearing 12
fruits 6, 12, 113, 165, 168
fry 65
fundamental 16, 90
fundamentalism 73
funerary 80
fungi 109
furnace 90
furnished 94
furs 116
future 22, 34, 92, 94

gaia 23
galen 70
gamos 99
garden 30, 126, 153
gardens 54, 146, 150
garment 25, 39
gas 167
gases 7
gellius 9
genealogia 6
genealogical 105
generic 38, 54, 56
genesis 48, 85, 90, 104, 105, 108, 153, 180
genii 114
genitals 45
genocidal 83
geometric 51
german 128
germanic 116, 121, 131, 159
germany 115, 116, 157
giant 13, 71, 105, 171
giants 104, 107, 110, 111
gilgamesh 85, 113
gingerbread 158
glaukopis 44
glaux 44
globe 11, 15, 94, 127, 140
gluten-free 169
gnomes 150
gnosis 71
gnostic 72, 73, 99, 141
gnostic-christian 71
gnostics 73, 80, 140
goat-totem 142
god 7, 10, 11, 12, 13, 14, 15, 22, 23, 24, 26, 27, 29, 30, 31, 33, 36, 38, 40, 41, 46, 48, 49, 51, 53, 54, 55, 56, 58, 60, 62, 63, 64, 66, 68, 73, 74, 75, 77, 79, 81, 82, 83, 84, 87, 92, 93, 95, 96, 97, 98, 104, 105, 107, 108, 109, 112, 113, 119, 120, 122, 123, 124, 125, 126, 127, 132, 140, 142, 151, 153, 157, 165, 166
god's 56, 87, 140, 165
goddess 19, 36, 37, 42, 43, 44, 46, 48, 57, 78, 79, 80, 113, 114, 146, 151, 153, 154, 180
goddess-mother 48
goddesses 54
godling 113
gods 9, 10, 11, 19, 20, 23, 24, 27, 30, 35, 38, 39, 56, 60, 66, 67, 71, 91, 109, 113, 120, 132, 139, 143, 144, 150, 152, 180
goethe 16
gold 8, 15, 16, 22, 24, 39, 46, 47, 52, 86, 98, 154
gold-leaf 79
goldmaking 87
golds 116
goldsmith 47
gorgoneion 72
gospel 73, 115
grain 168
grain-growing 19
granaries 65
gray-eyed 44
greece 6, 24, 29, 36, 44, 53, 54, 70, 78, 143, 154, 157, 176
greek 14, 17, 29, 30, 35, 36, 37, 39, 40, 43, 44, 45, 48, 50, 54, 55, 71, 73, 78, 79, 97, 113, 120, 142, 144, 145, 150, 151, 152, 153, 154, 180
griffins 30
guthrie 20, 23, 180
ha'elohim 108
hadad 55
haddon 116
hag 157

hagar 65
hagia 80
halloween 81
hallowmas 81
hallucigenic 144
hallucinations 143, 150, 151
hallucinogenic 29, 152, 153, 154, 155, 157
hammadi 73, 74, 80
haoma 120
harran 76
hathor 57
headdress 57
heaven 15, 18, 41, 45, 46, 47, 73, 85, 92, 106, 107, 109, 110, 113, 122, 131, 132, 133, 139, 144, 148, 151, 165, 166
heavens 15, 40, 55, 56, 103, 109, 122, 126, 128, 132
hebrew 9, 33, 35, 37, 48, 49, 64, 71, 74, 76, 101, 104, 107, 108, 149, 153, 155, 156
hebrews 49, 50, 65, 75
hecale 18
hecalesian 18
hecaline 18
hecalus 18
hecate 44
heifer 43
heinrich 12, 82, 123, 180
hekate 23
heliocentric 70
hellenes 80
hellenic 44, 46
hellenism 92
hellenistic 53, 83, 92
hephaestus 19
hera 20, 24, 44, 45, 80, 103
hera's 78, 79
heracles 17, 18, 55

heralds 18
herb 85
herbalism 133
herbs 113
hercules 29
herd 78, 161
herds 42
heresy 62
heretic 60, 62
heretics 74
herkyna 20, 21, 24
herm 6
hermai 21
hermes 14, 46, 70, 72, 79, 85, 92
hermetic 15, 72, 90
hermeticism 70
hermetis 12
hermolaus 85
hermon 107
hero 13, 18, 45, 69, 81, 85, 97, 128, 132, 143, 158
herodotus 19, 27, 40, 68, 97, 180
heroes 17, 18, 58, 88, 108, 158
heroin 139
herophilus 69, 70
herwa 78
hesiod 10, 112
hesperides 153
hesychius 10, 45
hgh 168
hierarchical 56
hieroglyphic 64
hieros 99
high 39, 40, 41, 65, 72, 73, 74, 101, 108, 109, 118, 152, 155, 157, 160, 170, 174, 176
hill 45, 47, 80
hillsides 160
hilltop 47
hindu 42, 119

hipparchus 69
hippo 105
hippodameia 18
hiram 53, 55, 112
hirsch 59
hissarlik 46, 47
hittite 45
hoghelande 8
holy 10, 40, 49, 56, 77, 81, 83, 94, 98, 112, 116, 117, 120, 149, 151, 165
honey 22, 29, 30, 31, 79, 113
honey-cake 23
honey-cakes 23
honey-drink 30
honey-man 80
honeyed 25
hooves 81, 143
horeb 75
horebheb 60
horemheb 60, 61
hormanuthi 86
horned 41, 42, 81, 129, 132
horse-totem 142
horus 27, 84, 86, 87, 92, 96
hyaluronan 160
hyaluronate 160
hyaluronic 160, 171
hydrogen 174
hylas 37
hylealischen 93
hypatia 72
hyperactivity 174
hyperenor 88
ia 85
ia-ion 72
iahu 85
iaion 72
iasius 140
iberia 52, 53

iberian 53
ibotenic 16, 68, 104
ice 166
ice-age 164
iceland 153
icon 97
iconography 53, 130
ida 10, 48
idaean 10
idols 44, 46, 77
ignatius 94
ignis 121
iliaster 16, 93
ilion 47
illuminated 8
illumination 151
illuminator 81
immortality 6, 7, 38, 85, 124, 130, 131, 133, 143
impurities 93
inachus's 42
incanstant 14
incest 54
incinerated 70
incineratio 97
incorporeal 94
india 29, 35, 36, 47, 65, 142, 143, 155
indian 50, 152, 153
indians 58, 144
indica 43
indigenous 40, 129
indoles 152
inebriate 121
inertia 143
infinite 8, 72, 90
infinity 5, 89
ingest 4, 49, 126, 168, 171
initiate 82, 141
initiated 18, 60

initiates 38, 123
initiation 18, 81, 82, 83, 127, 128, 129, 132
inquisitions 83
insanity 7
insulin 168, 170
io 42, 43, 45, 80
ion 36
ipu-wer 52
iran 30
iraq 42, 165
irenaeus 83, 105, 106
irish 45, 67, 149
iron 15, 41, 46, 47, 128, 163, 173, 174, 175, 177
isaac 64
isaiah 59
ischys 45
ishmaelites 65
ishtar 36, 78, 85
isis 27, 52, 66, 71, 83, 84, 86, 96, 104
isis-ra-elohim 104
islamic 120
island 50, 51, 73, 153
isles 150
israel 33, 53, 58, 77, 104, 109, 112
israeli 112, 113
israelite 40, 77, 112, 113
israelites 35, 41, 64, 75, 76, 77, 78
istar 37
italian 50, 63
italy 27
ivy 151, 156
ivyale 142
ixias 45
ixion 45
ixion's 143
jacob 22, 33, 104
jade 46

jadwiga 159
jadzia 159
jaga 158
jagusia 159
japan 175
japanese 146, 160
jehovah 9, 13
jelly 160
jeremiah 35, 112
jerusalem 53, 77, 112, 147
jesus 4, 13, 31, 35, 63, 67, 72, 81, 82, 84, 86, 90, 99, 104, 106, 119, 120, 132, 133, 139, 141
jethro 75
jewelry 47
jewels 154
jewish 58, 74, 76, 105, 108, 156
jews 44, 59, 65, 78, 105, 149
jibrâ 165, 166
jig-saw 67
john 12, 39, 82, 85, 128
jonah 39
jordan 42
josef 30, 81, 180
joseph 65
josephus 55, 105
josiah 77
jove 9, 151
jovis 9
jubilee 107
jubilees 107
judaeo-christian 148
judah 77
judaism 105, 106, 132
judas 146
jude 106
judeo-christian 67
judges 82, 112, 156
juice 73, 85, 86, 151, 152, 156, 164, 173

juices 88, 96, 98, 120
julius 105
jung 4, 5, 12, 13, 15, 50, 89, 91, 95, 121, 180
juniper 52
jupiter 9, 11, 35
ka 61
kaaba 159
kabbalah 35
karnak 60
kaufmann 97
kawamura 175
ketuvim 112
key 40, 59, 62, 76, 125, 126, 127, 130, 145
keyhole 158
keys 4, 71, 122
khai-t 53
khani 43
khattusha 85
khrestos 71
khunrath 12, 89, 93
kielce 158
king 19, 20, 37, 40, 43, 44, 46, 53, 55, 57, 61, 65, 67, 68, 71, 72, 77, 79, 82, 99, 100, 112, 132, 143, 144, 154, 157
kings 17, 38, 40, 53, 60, 71, 77, 82, 112, 114, 116, 143, 149
kippur 74
kish 41
kiya 67
kiyah 67
kohen 112
kokabel 110
kondakis 176
kontur 175
korjaks 152, 153
koryak 124
kossyra 50

kronos 5, 20, 24, 30, 95
l'homme 155
labrys 48
labyrinth 19, 23, 179
lactobacillus 172
lady 51, 57, 78, 179
lagourani's 165
lake 71
lamb 76
lamentations 52, 54
lapidem 9
lapis 5, 6, 7, 12, 13, 89
lapis-christ 13
latin 37, 54, 67, 85
latvia 114
lauzforn 149
lebadeia 20, 24
lebadia 43
lebanon 52
leprous 77
lethargy 176
lethe 21, 25
leto 27, 83
levi 74
lewes 65
libation 30
liber 30
libera 31
liberation 72, 156
liberia 31
librum 94
libya 53
libyan 97
light 12, 15, 22, 40, 48, 50, 59, 61, 71, 81, 83, 96, 133, 168
lightning 56, 92, 103, 121, 122, 144, 151, 152
lilim 44
lilith 44, 72, 84
limb 175

lineage 64, 111
linen 21, 25
linguist 85
linus 37
lion 14, 61, 78, 93, 166
lisichka 156
lithuania 114
liver 4, 8, 163, 174, 175
loaves 68
lonely 97
lord 6, 11, 14, 42, 54, 56, 58, 75, 104, 108, 112
lore 17, 115, 119, 131
lotus 68, 69
love 31, 66, 96, 118, 122, 123, 141, 147, 148
loyola 94
lucian 54
luna 16
luxor 60
lycurgus 143
lydia 29
lymphatic 161
lyon 140
lysa 158
lysidice 18
macedonian 159
macrocosmi 13
madonna 83, 84
maenad 142
maenads 68, 142, 143, 144, 151
magdalene 63, 67, 141
magic 67, 81, 82, 112, 118, 119, 121, 123, 128, 159, 180
magical 32, 69, 80, 84, 85, 120, 123, 124, 150, 158
magicians 153
magistery 91
magistrates 105
magnesium 169, 170, 177

magnum 23, 29
maiden 42, 129
maidens 44
majorca 145, 146
malak 165
malta 50, 55
maltese 55
malâk 165, 166
mammoth 166
man-fish 38
mana 109
mandaean 41, 76
mandrake 91
manganese 174, 175, 176, 177
manhood 156
manna 120, 155
mantle 39
march 31
marduk 85, 113
mari 47
mary 63, 67, 83, 84, 141
masatec 144
masonry 21, 82
materia 5, 12, 89, 90, 94, 96, 98, 120
matriarchal 113
matriarchy 113
matristic 140
maya 83
mead 29, 30
mead-orgies 148
meat 20, 24, 96, 163, 167, 177
meat-eater 174
medea 29
medica 90
medicine 6, 56, 69, 71, 98, 169
medusa 97
megiddo 85
melancholy 6
melchisedek 93

melchizedek 101
melissa 80
melisseus 80
meliteion 30
melkarth 29
melqarth 55, 56
melt 114, 124
melting 166
melusina 83, 84
melusinian 90
membrane 118
memory 21, 22, 25, 59, 60, 152
memphis 61
menander 55
meningitis 154
menses 85
menstrual 129
mental 70, 147, 176
mephistopheles 16
merchants 52
mercurial 98
mercurialis 121
mercuriall 9
mercurii 97
mercurius 5, 13, 14, 15, 16, 87, 89, 92, 93, 95, 121
mercury 8, 14, 71
mery 67
mesopotamia 51, 113
mesopotamian 41
messiah 10, 27, 31, 36, 71, 72
metabolism 171
metal 46, 53
metallurgy 82
metals 15, 46, 52, 53, 110, 177
metaphor 82
metasomatosis 94
methe 29, 30
methy 29, 30
methyein 29

methyskein 29
mexican 153, 154, 157
mexicans 34, 35
mexico 35, 144
mice 175
microcosm 13, 15, 75, 93, 95, 98
microcosmi 13
microscope 103, 122
microscopic 47
midea 46, 97
midian 75
midianites 75
miletos 78
milk 114, 151, 152, 153, 157, 168, 170, 177
milteios 78
miltiades 17
mind 7, 14, 15, 16, 17, 20, 25, 31, 49, 116, 117, 123, 128, 132, 139, 141
mineral 93, 160, 169
mineralium 6
minoan 48
minos 18, 19, 43, 44
minotaur 19
mirror 13, 45, 83, 143
miscarriage 108
mistletoe 45
mistress 57, 78
mitochondria 169, 170, 171
mitra 40
mnemosyne 21, 22, 25, 71
mobads 82
moist 5, 6, 14, 16, 89, 94, 98
moisture 92, 94, 98
molecule 160, 174
monad 98
mongol 152
monkeys 175
monks 72

monogamy 80
monograms 38
monomania 58
monotheism 59, 112
monotheist 62, 67
monster 64
monstrous 97, 158
monuments 33, 50, 83
moon 7, 8, 41, 42, 43, 45, 71, 76, 83, 93, 94, 95, 110, 116
moon-being 44
moon-cow 19, 42, 43
moon-deficients 76
moon-goddess 42, 43, 45
moon-goddess's 43
moon-goddesses 43
moon-priestess 44, 46
moon-triad 44, 80
mortar 157
mortificatio 89
moses 58, 59, 63, 64, 67, 74, 75, 112
moshe 105
moshiy'a 71
moslem 148
mother 15, 18, 19, 27, 31, 36, 61, 67, 72, 79, 80, 83, 84, 97, 113, 132, 146, 148, 149, 151, 159
mother-goddess 40, 113
motya 50
mount 10, 46, 52, 56, 62, 74, 78, 79, 85, 107, 156
mountain 10, 14, 21, 23, 40, 41, 48, 56, 75, 93, 158
mountains 40, 41, 47, 118, 120, 158
mouth 22, 71, 144, 158
mucus 169
multi-ethnic 112
mummy 61
muscaria 5, 9, 14, 16, 29, 32, 35, 37, 50, 68, 71, 88, 90, 94, 95, 99, 103, 104, 117, 118, 120, 125, 127, 131, 132, 140, 143, 151, 153, 154, 155, 156, 157, 178
muscle 162, 176
muscular 143, 147, 175
musee 155
muses 146
museum 27, 69, 70, 72
mushroom 5, 7, 9, 12, 16, 29, 31, 32, 35, 45, 48, 49, 50, 64, 67, 73, 74, 81, 82, 83, 84, 86, 88, 89, 97, 98, 104, 109, 117, 118, 119, 120, 121, 122, 123, 126, 127, 129, 130, 132, 139, 141, 142, 143, 144, 147, 148, 149, 150, 151, 152, 153, 154, 155, 157, 180
mushroom-eating 149
mushroom-god 144
mushroom-juice 156
mushrooms 3, 5, 7, 19, 31, 42, 45, 74, 81, 82, 103, 109, 110, 117, 118, 119, 120, 121, 122, 123, 126, 127, 129, 130, 132, 139, 142, 143, 144, 146, 147, 148, 149, 150, 152, 153, 155, 156, 157, 163, 180
music 114
muslims 165
mycelium 12, 32, 93, 120, 122
mycenae 43, 47, 79, 97, 144, 147, 157
mycenaean 18, 46, 48, 49, 78, 180
mycenean 151
mycologist 155
mycophages 148
mycophagous 155, 157
mycophobes 148, 149, 156
mycophobic 149, 157
mycorrhizal 122
mycos 97

mylitta 40
mylius 5, 89, 94
mysteries 10, 15, 18, 29, 68, 70, 72, 79, 83, 84, 86, 90, 99, 117, 143, 144, 154
mystery 11, 34, 61, 71, 81, 91, 95, 99, 120, 125, 165
mystic 70, 151
mystical 11, 43, 73, 124, 125
mysticism 13, 14, 73
myth 23, 36, 37, 43, 52, 58, 59, 70, 79, 96, 97, 114, 119, 141, 154
mythology 46, 54, 58, 59, 70, 84, 145, 180
nabataean 41
nabateans 41
nabisco 104
nachman 105
nachmanides 106
nag 73, 74, 80
nagas 38
napal 107
nast 115, 117
nebmaatre 61
nebo 58
nectar 30, 139, 142, 143, 144, 150
nefertiti 63, 67
negates 170
nemesis 43, 80
nephilim 62, 105, 107, 108, 110
nepthys 66
nero's 150
nessus 143
netherlands 164
neurological 173, 176
neurotoxicity 175
nevi'im 112
night 17, 20, 21, 25, 30, 39, 42, 44, 75, 76, 114, 115, 121, 125, 158
nightmares 151

nike 48
nile 6, 51, 68, 89
ninou 43
niphal 107
nisa 30
nitrian 72
nkjv 104
noah 38
nomads 157
norman 116
norse 124, 143, 148, 153
north 49, 50, 52, 60, 62, 114, 115, 121, 148, 149, 157
noster 121
nostra 86
nsha 36
nubia 61, 62
nuit 80
numerology 142
nusa 36
nusha 36
nutrients 160, 162, 171, 176
nutrition 160, 161, 170
nuts 167, 168
nymph 42, 43, 79
nymph-goddess 80
nymphs 79
nysa 79
oak 46, 68
oak-cult 45
oak-goddess 45
oak-king 45
oaks 30
oannes 38, 39
oath 9, 106
oaxaca 144
occult 71
occulta 14
occultist 38
ocean 86

ochai 105
october 151
odysseus 85
ogdoad 5, 89, 91
ogelius 8
oil 5, 21, 25, 56, 89, 141, 167
oily 5, 89
ointment 141
olen 10
olenos 10, 11
olive 69
olympian 43, 150
olympic 30, 143
olympiodorus 87, 97
omega 95, 177
omnipotent 64
omphalos 6
opium 85
opus 6, 7, 13, 29, 89, 91
oracle 6, 20, 21, 24, 25
oracles 24, 26
oracular 24, 80, 88
orchard 153, 154
oreithyia 114
organ 123, 169
organic 32, 95
organism 160
organs 161, 162, 163, 169, 170
orgasm 123
orgiastic 40, 46, 79, 80
oriental 30
orientalists 38
orifices 162
origen 105
oristano 51
orpheus 59, 68, 72
orphic 59, 143
osarsiph-moses 59
osiris 27, 29, 35, 39, 45, 52, 66, 87,

88, 96, 104, 132
ostanes 4, 6, 91
osteoporosis 170
ovid 10, 31, 36
owl 44, 45, 72
owl-eyed 44
ox-eyed 45
ox-goad 143
oxford 145, 153
oxide 174
oxygen 171, 173, 174
pagan 31, 36, 37, 77, 81
paganism 11, 31, 123, 132
pagans 32, 139
palace 85
palaeo-siberians 152
palenque 35
palestine 44, 154
palestinian 156
palisade 158
palladium 46
pallas 46
palm 83, 124
pan 81, 132
panacea 6
panaeolus 143, 154
pancreas 175
pandora 83
panopolis 80
pantelleria 50
pantheon 53, 60
pantophthalmos 14
papal 11, 81
papilionaceus 143
papyri 67
papyrus 73, 99
parable 14
paracelsan 16
paracelsus 16, 89, 90, 92
paradise 84, 99, 127, 153, 154, 155,

157, 165, 166
paradises 153
paralysed 22
paralyzed 25
parkinson's 174
parmenides 98
parthia 30
pasah 76
paschal 76
pashupati 42
pasta 168
pastoral 80
pasupati 42
patai 113
patriarch 65, 67, 81
patriarchal 11, 43, 113
patriarchy 6, 30, 113
pausanias 20, 23, 24
pausanicus 157
pelican 12, 16
pellicanicum 12
peloponnese 17, 157
peloponnesian 17
pelops 17, 18
pelorus 88
peristalsis 69
peroxide 174
persephone 54
perseus 96, 97, 144, 157
persia 5, 29, 30, 81, 91, 180
persian 40
persians 58
pesah 75, 76
pestle 157
petasios 87
petra 41, 78
phallic 46
phalloides 150
pharaoh 58, 62, 65, 103
pharaohs 62, 65

pharisees 4
pharmacological 72
pharmacology 69
pharmakon 72
phenomenon 143
pheonician 56
pheonissa 42
philadelphus 99
philistine's 156
philistines 147, 156
philo 53, 56, 105
philosopher 72, 94, 95
philosopher's 5, 71, 86
philosophers 13, 14, 15, 70, 71, 86, 91, 93, 113
philosophic 5, 14, 15, 89, 121
philosophical 6, 12, 73
philosophicus 7
philosophists 4
philosophorum 12, 16
philosophy 15, 89
phocica 10
phoenicia 29, 51, 53, 55
phoenician 35, 37, 49, 50, 51, 53, 54, 55, 112
phoenicians 29, 34, 48, 49, 50, 52, 53, 57, 112
phoenix 42, 78, 97
phoinike 49
phoinikes 49
phoinix 49
phonetic 37, 73
phonetically 38, 41
phoroneus 157
phoroneus's 157
phosphorus 177
phrygia 10, 29, 40
phryneus 157
phyllis 129
physical 39, 58, 70, 81, 92, 161

physics 69, 70
physiological 7, 174
physis 13
pillars 41, 46
pine 17, 91, 120, 122, 148, 155
pine-goddess 17
pinecone 27, 29, 31, 32, 33, 34
pines 114, 156
pistis 140
pitthea 17
pittheus 17, 18
plato 30
plato's 87, 98
plutarch 17, 26, 27, 30, 180
pneuma 86, 87, 94
po-ni-ki-ja 49
po-ti-ni-ja 179
po-yang 7
poison 15, 74, 149, 150, 156
poison-dripping 14
poisoning 7, 173, 176
poisonous 16, 74, 86, 88, 118, 148, 149, 157
poland 114
polish 158
poltergeists 146
polynesian 153
polytheism 53, 112
pomegranate 37
ponike 48
pope 31, 81
poppies 85
poppy-head 68
poros 30
porphyra 37
porphyry 30
porphyry's 99
poseidon 47, 48, 78
poseidon's 48
possession 23, 69

potassium 177
potatoes 160
potentate's 153
potidaea 48
potidan 48
praesus 80
prancer 122
prang 116
prawns 149
prayer 3
pre-agricultural 114
pre-civilized 140
pre-classical 143, 151
pre-death 141
pre-flood 105
pre-hellenic 43, 46, 78
pre-islamic 78
priest 10, 60, 63, 65, 72, 74, 101
priestess 144, 154
priestesses 154
priesthood 59, 60
priests 10, 21, 22, 25, 38, 39, 40, 59, 63, 70, 109, 149, 151, 152, 154, 159
prima 5, 12, 89, 94, 96, 98, 120
primeval 46, 85
primitive 30, 37, 46, 47, 66, 84, 148, 168
prince 59
principal 41, 51, 68, 87, 113
principalities 141
proclus 68
proetus 96
prohibitio 71
promethean 113
prometheus 113
prophecies 153
prophecy 23, 80, 128
prophesied 36, 94
prophesies 20

prophesying 141
prophet 10, 24, 109
prophetess 86
prophetic 72, 143
prophets 10, 23, 112
prostitution 54
prostrate 30
proto-israelite 47
proto-slavic 159
psalliotis 148
psalm 64
pseudepigraphic 106
pseudo-aquinas 8
psilocybe 144, 153, 154
psilocybin 5, 163
psychedelic 81, 82, 127, 132, 139, 140
psychic 7
psychoactive 29, 69
psychosis 13
ptolemais 72
ptolemies 69
ptolemy 69, 70, 99
puer 92
purification 35
purified 15, 18
purity 20, 158
purple 37, 164
purpose 16, 35, 112, 160
purpura 37
pyramid 92, 168, 173
pythagorean 92
python 88
qasim 91
qaush 41
qodcsh 56
qos 41
qos-allah 41
quadratus 5, 89
quash 41

quaternity 5, 89, 91
queen 77, 103, 113, 151
queen's 113
queen-bee 79, 80
queens 143
quinta 12
quintessence 13, 86
ra 53
rabbat 78
rabbi 59, 105
rabbinic 105, 106
rabbits 119
radical 94, 98, 169, 174
raiders 156
rain 84
rain-making 45, 80
rains 122
ram 20, 21
ramayana 42, 79
rape 46
rapes 46
rashi 105
rastafarian 67
rats 172, 173, 175
raven 128
raw 43, 59, 143
realm 131, 132
realms 124, 132
rebirth 125, 130, 131, 167
red 5, 13, 14, 15, 30, 33, 35, 36, 37, 38, 42, 43, 48, 49, 50, 64, 78, 91, 93, 97, 98, 104, 116, 117, 118, 121, 122, 126, 127, 128, 129, 149, 158, 164
red-coated 150
red-coloured 37
redeemer 13, 95, 96
redeeming 141
redemption 72, 89, 95
regeneration 31, 70

reindeer 118, 121, 122, 123, 124, 127, 128, 150, 157
reshef 53
retort 16
rhea 9, 48, 79, 80
rhesus 175
rhinoceros 166
rhodes 45
rhodius 23, 69
rhytons 30
rice 160
rites 18, 22, 24, 37, 40, 60, 68, 107, 139, 154
ritual 30, 45, 54, 55, 74, 85, 114, 141, 154, 155
ritually 19, 44, 45, 155
rituals 129, 139
robes 37, 113, 116
roman 9, 30, 31, 34, 35, 37, 50, 51, 54, 56, 72, 122
rome 9, 11, 36, 40, 50, 71, 112, 140, 147
roof 52, 118
rooftops 54
rosacrucians 14
rosarium 13
rosarius 13
rose 13, 14, 37, 68, 87, 110, 125
rose-coloured 13, 93
rose-gardener 13, 14
rosy-coloured 93
rotundum 97, 98
royal 23, 37, 44, 57, 58, 60, 61, 62, 69, 70, 77, 104, 109
rudra 42
ruha 77
ruska 98
russia 148, 151
russian 115, 117, 119, 128, 157, 159
russians 148, 156

russkie 159
sabbath 149
sabbaths 81, 158
saber-toothed 166
sacerdotal 39
sacrament 72, 120
sacramental 139, 140
sacraments 139
sacred 4, 6, 9, 10, 11, 20, 22, 25, 35, 37, 43, 45, 46, 48, 56, 57, 68, 71, 73, 78, 79, 82, 83, 84, 86, 99, 109, 113, 123, 128, 131, 132, 139, 141, 143, 144, 149, 150, 155, 156, 180
sacrifice 20, 24, 40, 43
sacrificed 17, 35, 37, 50, 74, 78, 81, 141
sacrifices 20, 21, 24, 25, 40, 45
sacrificial 74, 129, 154
sacrificially 78
sages 105, 153
sailors 154
saint's 81
saints 74, 133, 154
salamandrine 90
salnson 156
salt 6, 16, 93, 169, 177
samael 74
samaritan 76
samhain 81
samos 70
samson 147, 156
samson's 156
samuel 109
sanctuaries 51, 55
sanctuary 22, 23, 50, 54, 55, 56
sandals 97
sanskrit 42, 72, 150
santa 115, 116, 117, 118, 119, 120, 121, 123, 124, 127, 128, 129, 130,

132, 133
sapientiae 93
sapientum 13
sapphire 5
sappho 151
saracens 155
sarah 65
sarcophagus 80
sardinia 50, 53, 55, 56
sargon 58, 59
sariel 110
satan 81, 82, 95, 132, 133, 165
sativa 99, 103
saturday 116, 149
saturn 9, 10, 11, 30, 92, 95, 97
saturnalia 35
saturnine 9, 93, 97
saturninus 9
saturnus 9
satyrs 142, 143
saul 67, 109
savior 13, 84
saviour 7, 36, 71
scaliger 93
scaly 38
scandinavia 153
scapegoat 74, 78, 81
scarab 41
scarlet 150, 152, 153
scarlet-capped 147
scepter 35, 79, 103
scorpions 82
scotland 151
scribes 4
script 41, 64
scripture 106
scritch-owl 44
scrolls 73, 82, 85
scrying 34
scythian 86

scythians 114
se'ir 74
sea 12, 38, 39, 52, 62, 66, 82, 85, 91, 92, 93
sea-faring 43
sea-serpent 113
sea-water 93
seafarers 48
seafood 167
seir 41, 62, 74, 77, 78
seir-edom 40
self-initiates 7
semele 97, 151
semen 19, 84, 128
semetic 14, 56
semetic-speaking 47
semi-nomadic 121
semi-suppressed 73
semieniatka 114
semiramis 31
semitic 54, 153
semjaza 106, 110
senate 160, 161
senex 92
sense 56, 76, 80, 88, 98, 104, 108, 109, 110, 119, 123, 125, 141
senses 15, 30, 107
sera 41
serbian 159
serpent 8, 38, 57, 58, 63, 64, 72, 84, 88, 98, 140, 153, 157
serpent-crown 144
serpent-drawn 37
serpent-tailed 114
serpents 23, 38, 119
servius 35
sesephus 45
set 10, 22, 24, 38, 52, 86, 87, 96, 119, 125, 126, 145, 147, 161
seth 54, 66, 105

sexism 132
·sexual 54, 123, 128, 147
sexuality 133
seymour 34
shaddai 75
shamaim 54, 56
shaman 71, 84, 85, 91, 118, 119, 120, 121, 122, 124, 125, 128, 131, 132
shaman's 124, 127, 128, 131, 140
shamanic 17, 81, 112, 121, 122, 123, 124, 125, 127, 129, 130, 133
shamanism 6, 30, 76, 91, 98, 123, 127, 129, 130, 131, 133, 140, 180
shamanistic 84
shamans 35, 121, 123, 130
shamsiel 110
shapur 81
shara 41
shasu 40, 41, 62, 75
she-goat 80
shenoute 80
shepherds 43, 82
sherbet 148
shifting 123, 124, 130, 131, 132, 167
shining 96
shiva 42
shlomo 105
shulamite 147
shunemite 156
siculus 53, 68, 80
sidon 43, 49
sidonians 53
silurist 153
sin 36, 42, 95, 106, 140
sin-bearer 10, 36
sin-bearing 5, 9, 10
sins 10, 78, 81, 104
sirai 50

sisyphus 45
skull 158
skulls 130, 158
sky 45, 56, 124, 131, 132
slavic 115, 117, 158, 159
slavicized 159
slavs 157
slovak 158
slovene 158
smenkh 61
smenkhare 58, 63, 67
smenkhkare 60, 61
snails 141
snake 19, 50, 71, 94
snake's 71
snake-kings 38
snake-like 154
snakes 4, 25, 50, 82, 154
sodality 148
sodium 177
sol 16, 67, 92
solar 27, 58, 63, 65, 97
soleb 61, 62
solomon 53, 65, 77, 112, 147, 156
solomon's 49, 53, 112
solstice 68, 81, 128, 129, 130
soma 29, 119, 120, 121, 127, 150, 151, 152, 155
sophia 93
sophic 71
sophists 90
sophokles 70
sorcerers 123
spain 51, 55, 145, 148
spains's 116
spaniards 35
sphere 87, 101
spheres 86
spherical 94, 97
spirit 6, 13, 16, 23, 76, 77, 85, 86,

89, 93, 94, 95, 97, 98, 104, 109,
131, 140, 158
spirits 114
spiritual 7, 8, 39, 64, 70, 86, 87, 89,
94, 98, 123, 129
spirituality 73, 178
spiritus 92, 97
spores 103, 109, 122
spritual 16
stars 95, 115
statue 25, 61
statues 40, 60
statuettes 45
stela 41
stone 5, 6, 7, 8, 9, 10, 11, 13, 41,
45, 46, 67, 68, 69, 71, 82, 85, 86,
89, 91, 93, 95, 97, 155
stones 5, 9, 11, 91, 99, 110, 180
stoning 82
strawberries 149
stropharia 154
sudan 61, 62
sugar 139, 169, 171, 172, 176
sugar-filled 167
sugar-free 169
sulcis 51
sulphur 16, 87, 89
sumerian 42, 85, 113, 153
sun 8, 11, 15, 38, 42, 45, 59, 60, 62,
63, 66, 67, 68, 71, 76, 82, 83, 87,
93, 95, 97, 110, 125, 130, 141, 158,
167
sun's 15, 141
sun-bull 46
sun-disk 64
sun-god 45
sun-w 58
sunlight 167
sunset 75
surya 29

sussex 65
swaddled 5, 10, 11
swaddling 9
swallowed 24
sware 106
swastika 47
sweden's 116
swietokrzyskie 158
syeg 149
synesius 72
synthetic 162, 163
syracuse 70
syria 29, 51, 54
syria-iraq 47
syrian 56
syro-palestinian 51
ta'us 165
taboo 37, 143, 149, 150, 155
taboos 149, 150
tabor 156
tail 19, 39, 71
tails 147, 156
tammuz 11, 30, 31, 33, 35, 37
tanakh 108
tantalus's 143
tau 33
taurus 19
taxing 169
tea 139
tearing 89, 142, 144
tehom 85
tepentitla 144
terra-cotta 44
tertullian 105
tetrasomia 92
thammuz 35, 36, 37
the-one-on-high 124
theban 60
thebes 29, 60
themistocles 17

theobald 8
theocratic 127
theocritus 69
theogon 10
theology 63
theon 72
theophrastus 70
theseus 17, 18, 19
thessalian 143
thigh 19, 151, 152
tho 125
thor 124
thoth 70
thrace 78, 79
thraco-libyan 79
thunder 121, 122
thunder-god 45
thunderbolt 48, 68, 103
thyone 151
thyroid 170
tiamat 85, 113
til 47
timaeus 87, 98
timarchus 26
timber 52
tincture 5, 6, 13
tinctures 110
tinder 45, 97
titanic 107
titans 79
tlaloc 144, 153
tlalocan 153
tlalóc 157
tlalócan 157
toad 144, 156, 157
toad-man 157
toadheaded 153
toadstool 144
toadstools 149, 156
toast 168

tobacco 139
tongue 9
tonsure 54
tophet 50, 51
torah 112
torch 83
torches 147, 156
tortures 82
totem 130
totemic 112
totemistic 46
tractatus 12
train 39, 116
trance 25, 128
trance-dancing 122
trance-like 130
transcendental 144
treatise 8, 11, 54, 90, 96
treatises 121
tree 5, 6, 12, 32, 64, 71, 83, 84, 89,
91, 92, 93, 118, 120, 131, 132, 150,
159
tree-numen 83
treeless 157
trees 32, 42, 52, 68, 99, 114, 118,
122, 153, 154
tremor 176
triada 80
triangle 78
tribal 40, 114, 155
tribe 74, 155, 165
tribes 33, 104
tribesmen 142
tribute 18
trident 48
trigonometry 69
trinity 100
triptolemus 37, 43, 154
triptolemus's 154, 155
trismegistus 70, 72, 85, 92

troezen 17
trojan 44, 150
trophonios 20, 21, 22, 23, 24, 25, 26
tsarion 67
tumors 171
tuna 168
tunic 21
tunisia 50
turba 12, 67, 98
turbae 94
tut-ankh-aten 61
tutankhamen 63, 64, 65, 66
tutankhamen's 67
tutankhamun 41, 60, 61, 62, 64, 65, 180
tutankhaten 61
tuthmosis 63, 65
tyre 49, 53, 55, 56, 112
tyrian 53, 112
tâwûs 165, 166
udaeus 88
ufology 50
ugarit 56
ukraine 114
ukrainian 159
ulcers 168
unconscious 22, 126
unhallucinogenic 155
unicorn 43
uraeus 57
uranian 40
ush-tar 85
uterus 85
utopian 73
uz 74, 78
vampiric 107
vampirism 107
vase 43, 143
vases 44, 45

vegetarians 176
vegetativus 92
veil 118
versipellis 14
victim-man 36
vinaigrette 168
vinegar 98
vines 147, 156
viniculture 30
viper 88
virgin 27, 31, 71, 83, 84
visio 12
vision 94, 126
visionary 124, 125, 126, 127
visions 25, 26, 34, 92, 97, 143, 144
vivus 7
vixen 123
vizier 61, 65
vulva 44
war 71, 73, 115, 150
warfare 112
warrior 131
warts 156, 157
wasps 68
water 5, 11, 12, 14, 21, 27, 38, 39, 42, 70, 82, 83, 85, 86, 87, 89, 91, 92, 93, 94, 95, 96, 97, 98, 120, 141, 144, 153, 157, 160, 168, 171, 172, 174, 175, 176, 177
water-carrier 59
water-goddess 48
water-lilies 68
watercolour 8
waters 71, 85, 97, 120
wheat 164, 165, 166, 168, 169, 173, 176
whisky 151
white 5, 21, 37, 42, 43, 46, 64, 80, 83, 86, 91, 93, 116, 117, 118, 121, 122, 125, 127, 128, 129, 146, 148,

150, 157, 158, 164, 169, 173
white-spotted 150
whole-wheat 168
wind 114, 118, 125, 126, 169
wine 29, 30, 79, 142, 147, 152, 156
winged 14, 31, 63, 85, 87, 88, 97
wingless 14
wings 44, 48, 53, 97
winter 36, 99, 128, 129, 130
wisdom 17, 27, 38, 96, 98, 124,
126, 131, 133, 142, 161
witch 109, 123, 159
witchcraft 123
witches 123, 133, 158
wives 104, 106, 107, 108
wolves 166
woman 44, 49, 66, 83, 123, 159,
168
womb 13, 19, 71
women 19, 36, 40, 54, 80, 105, 109,
110, 111, 114, 141, 151, 155, 170
women's 123
womenfolk 142
wood 35, 52, 82
wooded 48
woodland 37
woods 148, 149
wool 3, 19, 152
woolly 166
world-creating 13
world-hence 154
world-tree 91

worlds 125, 131, 132
worship 25, 27, 43, 50, 51, 54, 55,
56, 57, 59, 63, 64, 67, 75, 76, 77,
78, 82, 105, 113, 132, 140, 144
worshipped 17, 21, 27, 35, 36, 40,
42, 60, 66, 80, 83, 109, 142, 153
worshippers 29, 40, 76, 78, 152
xenophon 180
xisuthrus 38
yahweh 40, 41, 62, 74, 75, 77
yehawmilk's 57
yellow 119, 151, 164
yhw 62
yield 42, 86, 87
yitzchaki 105
yogic 128
yurba 76
zadok 101
zagreus 43, 68
zarathustra 97
zenobia 70
zentralbibliothek 8
zeus 6, 18, 20, 24, 27, 30, 40, 43,
45, 46, 47, 48, 55, 56, 78, 79, 80,
103, 113, 151, 152
zinc 176
zlotkin 175
zoomorphic 51
zosimos 93, 95, 97, 98
zu-en 42
zürich 8

Made in the USA
San Bernardino, CA
02 April 2014